Volume 25

No.
3. Representative American Speeches: 1952-1953. A. C. Baird. $1.75.

Volume 24

No.
1. Political Ethics and the Voter. T. A. Rousse. $1.75.

3. Representative American Speeches: 1951-1952. A. C. Baird. $1.75.

No.
6. Latin America in the Cold War. W. M. Daniels. $1.75.

Volume 23

No.
2. Representative American Speeches: 1950-1951. A. C. Baird. $1.75

Volume 22

No.
3. Representative American Speeches: 1949-1950. A. C. Baird. $1.75.

Volume 20

No.
5. Federal World Government. J. E. Johnsen. $1.50.

Volume 18

No.
3. Representative American Speeches: 1944-1945. A. C. Baird. $1.25

THE REFERENCE SHELF

Vol. 30 No. 6

AIRWAYS OF AMERICA

Edited by
POYNTZ TYLER

THE H. W. WILSON COMPANY
NEW YORK 1958

PN 4181
R 33

PREFACE

Ever since his creation man has envied the birds and tried to imitate their flight. The story of Daedalus and Icarus in Greek mythology is doubtless based on the failure of one such attempt and both the folklore and history of every land are filled with similar accounts of man's efforts to conquer the air. In the six-teenth century a Chinese mandarin attempted to fly in a kite chair powered by forty-seven gunpowder rockets, and the publication of Leonardo da Vinci's complete works in 1930 revealed that this protean genius had designed over 450 years ago an "aerial screw" that is a direct forebear of the modern helicopter. It could have flown, if built, but its inadequate spring motor would have reduced it to the status of an interesting toy. Until the arrival of the internal combustion engine—the first to produce enough power to lift more than its own weight—experiments with heavier-than-air machines were ordained to failure, and man first got off the ground by means of the balloon.

In 1783 the Montgolfier brothers of France, Joseph Michel and Jacques Etienne, inflated a large linen bag over a fire and then released it. The bag, 105 feet in circumference, rose "to a great height" and traveled nearly two miles before falling. This was the first balloon, and on its second flight it carried three passengers—a sheep, a cock, and a duck. All returned to earth safely and uninjured save the cock: he had been kicked by the sheep to become aviation's first casualty. The first man to follow these barnyard pioneers was Jean François Pilatre de Rozier, superintendent of Louis XVI's natural history collection. He ascended in 1783 in a captive balloon filled with heated air and later, with the Marquis d'Arlandes, in a free balloon kept buoy-ant by the burning of chopped straw in a brazier suspended under the bag.

Man has been increasingly airborne ever since but it is the near-tragedy of aviation that its greatest development and greatest use has been by the military. Count Ferdinand von Zeppelin is so irrevocably connected in the public mind with the huge, rigid, lighter-than-air ships bearing his name—the airships that bombed London during the first World War—that few remember him as being the true father of commercial air transport. Beginning in 1910 his fleet of Zeppelins maintained a regular passenger service between Friedrichshafen and Düsseldorf and carried over 17,000 passengers before they and their inventor were mobilized into the German army in 1914. In each of the two great wars that followed the first successful flight of heavier-than-air craft by the Wright brothers in 1903, aviation advanced with a speed that would have been impossible during peace; but the only lasting benefit of that wartime development has been its quick conversion to the ways and needs of peace.

So this book is not concerned with the airplane as a weapon. It is concerned solely with the airplane as an instrument of trade and commerce and with the men and women who have made it —in little more than half a century—the predominant means of public transportation in the United States. Aviation's rise to that position has been so swift—so interrupted by war and so goaded by war—that it has scarcely had time to write its own history. The present volume makes no pretense of so doing. It is a collection of articles from various sources that has been compiled in the hope that readers of the whole will gain knowledge and appreciation of the vast aerial traffic that enters daily into their lives and sight. To the writers and publishers of those articles the editor is deeply grateful for permission to reproduce their work.

POYNTZ TYLER

October 1958

CONTENTS

I. FROM THE GROUND UP

EDITOR'S INTRODUCTION

American commercial aviation was born on January 1, 1914, when Mayor Abram Crump Pheil of St. Petersburg, Florida, became the first passenger on the first passenger airline in the United States—the St. Petersburg-Tampa Airboat Line. The plane was a Benoist flying boat, the pilot was Anthony ("Tony") Jannus, the round trip between terminals was forty-six miles and the fare was $400. A tourist named Noel Mitchell paid $175 to make the second trip and from then on—such is the price of novelty—the fare sank to an established price of ten dollars. In April, when the tourists returned north, the St. Petersburg-Tampa Airboat Line disappeared too.

The astonishing part of Mayor Pheil's flight is not its cost of nearly ten dollars a mile but the fact that he could make his entry into aviation history at such an early date. Not until 1908, five years after Kitty Hawk, was any practical use made of the airplane in this country. Between 1903 and 1908 inventors and experimenters held the spotlight, and from 1908 to 1915 the airplane was essentially a source of thrills. Daring young men flew through the air for sheer excitement, others went along for the ride, still others got their thrills vicariously by watching from the ground. Aerial acrobatics, occasionally fatal, served to awaken the public to the fact of aviation and to develop a corps of young fliers—like Tony Jannus—who were to play a major part in the subsequent development of air transport.

The government, not without misgivings, helped. The Army adopted the airplane for military use in 1909, when the first military aircraft was accepted by the Signal Corps, and gave its planes the baptism of battle during the 1916 expedition in Mexico against Pancho Villa. Bombs were dropped and aerial observers scouted the elusive foe. The first airmail bill was introduced in Congress on June 14, 1910, and between September 23 and October 2, 1911, during an air meet on Long Island, an aviator named Earle L. Ovington carried mail by air between Nassau Boulevard and Garden City Estates. Since Ovington had been sworn in as a postman for the occasion, the date of September 23, 1911, is now considered the birthday of airmail in the United States.

World War I demonstrated that an early practical use of the airplane would be military, and ushered in a period of technical advance in aviation and public adulation of the airman. From April 1917, when the United States entered the war, until the Armistice in 1918, over one and a quarter billion dollars was appropriated by the United States for military aircraft. An embarrassingly small number of planes were delivered by the infant aircraft industry (American airmen flew French and English planes almost exclusively). But during this nineteen-month period the number of flight training fields increased from 2 to 48; the number of aviation officers from 55 to 20,000; the number of aviation mechanics from 1300 to 175,000; the country's aircraft potential from 224 planes annually to 17,000. The era of the "barnstormers" was inevitable.

The typical barnstormer, trained to fly during the war and loving nothing else, purchased a surplus Curtis JN4D2 airplane —the famous "Jenny"—and went into business. More than anyone else in early aviation he became the model for modern airline personnel. He could not afford to take chances with his plane for it represented his capital investment; so he was careful. His livelihood depended on satisfied customers; so he was courteous and dependable. He sold flight. He was aviation's first salesman to the general public; the first to crusade for better airfields, beacon lights, aids to navigation, service for his airplane. He was the first to realize the need for aviation education and the first to do something about it.

It is from these men that Theodore H. White traces the rise of commercial aviation in the opening article of this section. In the six articles that follow it other writers introduce some of the men and women and methods that have contributed to that advance—the government agencies which supervise airline operations, the manufacturers who produce the planes, the crews and maintenance men who keep them flying and provide safety and amenity in travel by air.

The last four articles deal with the gigantic air traffic problem that now confronts the country. In "Traffic Jam" Wolfgang Langewiesche describes the scope and, given the number of planes involved, the inevitability of such an airborne tangle. Richard Witkin, in "When the Plane Falls," tells what happens in the wake of the equally inevitable collisions, and the concluding articles are concerned with the plans and instruments being evolved to prevent them.

FROM THE JENNY TO THE JET [1]

Somewhere, somehow, a reporter keeps telling himself as he talks of the new age ahead with the men of the aviation world, there should be a note of caution, of restraint. But there is not. For in the art of American industry—that curious blend of dream and common sense which restlessly shapes the changes in our life before the constraints of dollar-accounting and public relations counsel set in—the men of aviation have always been preeminent.

"This," said one veteran, "is the industry of hashish-eaters. Nothing will ever seem as crazy a dream, nothing will ever seem as high or dark as night-crossing the Alleghenies seemed in 1928. You have to look back at how far we've come to understand."

To be exact, you have to look back thirty years—to the sultry, pregnant summer of 1926, when commercial aviation first tried its wings.

That was the time when the airmail, unwanted child of the Post Office Department, flying the castoff Jennys and De Havillands of World War I, sped two planes a day east from San Francisco and two planes west from New York; each took two days en route. Man thought then that the art of aviation had reached a summit. Only a few years before, a mail pilot, Jack Knight, had become a hero flying the first night flight across America from Omaha to Chicago; farmers on the rolling plains had lighted bonfires to guide him through the storm and help

[1] From "Our Crowded Sky," article by Theodore H. White, author and foreign correspondent. *Collier's.* 138:26-36. August 31, 1956. Copyright 1956 by The Crowell-Collier Publishing Company. Reprinted by permission.

him prove it could be done. But now, in 1926, the Bureau of Lighthouses was maintaining light beacons on the airmail routes, new planes were developing, flight was becoming routine.

So routine had it become, in fact, that the government a year earlier, by the Kelly Act of 1925, had daringly thrown the air open to private enterprise. The Postmaster General, stipulated the act, should have the right to trace airmail routes across the map and then let contracts to any group of men bold enough to think they could make a profit by bidding for the right to fly mail. And thus, in the summer of 1926, it all began.

The names of these first post office routes—CAM 1 (Contract Air Mail 1), CAM 2, CAM 3 and so on—lie buried in the archives of Washington. But their dry code names still trace the roots and branches from which American commercial aviation was to flourish.

CAM 1 (the contract between New York and Boston) was the fief of a new company called Colonial Air Transport—chiefly interesting in retrospect because of its visionary young chieftain. Juan Trippe saw the whole round globe with its wide oceans as the airplane's realm. The staid Boston owners of Colonial did not agree with him, so young Trippe left to found another airline called Pan American Airways, whose ambition was to jump the ocean from Florida to Havana.

In this, the first of his major aviation wars, twenty-seven-year-old Juan Trippe clashed with an equally colorful young man named Eddie Rickenbacker, who was at that time a director of a company called Florida Airways. Rickenbacker was also desperately interested in getting the Florida-Havana airmail contract. When Trippe won, Florida Airways folded and Rickenbacker was not again to tap the lush travel market of Florida until eight years later. Then, in 1935, as new general manager of Eastern Air Lines, he salvaged the company from almost certain bankruptcy and rode the Florida vacationland boom to great fortune and profit.

In San Francisco, a young banker had become interested in airplanes and joined an outfit called Pacific Air Transport which had bid and won CAM 8, the contract between Los Angeles and Seattle. His name was William A. Patterson.

In the next few years, as PAT was merged with the ownership of CAM 5 (the high Rockies), CAM 18 (Chicago-San Francisco) and the New York-Chicago leg of National Air Transport, Patterson soared with it to manage the first all-air coast-to-coast route in the country. Today, as United Air Lines, the system he directs crisscrosses the entire northern half of the nation and reaches all the way to Hawaii.

Down in Texas, another young man fresh out of college was about to go to work for a speculator who had latched onto five or six beat-up planes and an airmail contract, all based on Fort Worth. This operation, known as Texas Air Transport, flew to Houston-Galveston-Brownsville, down the Gulf Coast. The young man was C. R. Smith. From his tin-roofed shed by the dirt strip of Fort Worth's field, he was to shake this line down to operating efficiency and rise with it, as New York interests linked it to other stump contracts, until it became American Airlines, biggest of them all, and he became its president.

Now that air travel is commonplace and its stocks and debentures are first-class investment material, the audacity of the men who flew the planes and the men who financed them has all but been forgotten. But those were the days when even CAM 9—the simple flight between Chicago and Minneapolis—was high adventure, and the first bidder on that contract, a bewhiskered pioneer named Charles Dickinson, folded in four months. Of the five planes with which he opened his line, four had crashed in three months. A hastily assembled company called Northwest Airlines replaced him with better luck—today its original Minneapolis-Chicago run reaches from New York to Tokyo.

The settled, middle-aged men who today sit behind the command desks of American aviation seem like any other businessmen. But all that they command they created in their own lifetime; when they talk of yesterday, they become young again, remembering how all the early triumphs were hand-hewn out of human ignorance.

There was the battle of weather. John Collings, who now bosses the far-flung lines of TWA, remembers the weather back in 1926 when he was flying in Detroit. His boss was Henry

Ford, who was already running a regular private service of one-a-day flights of spare parts from Detroit to Chicago in 1925.

"We had no weather service at all in those days," remembers Collings, "so when the hangar burned down on New Year's Day, 1926, we used our spare time to set up a weather system. Two of us got in a car and went to Chicago. We'd stop every now and then, pick out a Ford dealer and take him outside and point to the sky and say, 'See, when it's like this, we say it's clear, or, if it's like that, we say it's scattered, or broken, or socked in.' Then we'd say, 'If you can see down the hill, visibility is one mile; if you can see as far as the church, visibility is two miles; if you can see as far as you want, it's unlimited.' Then we'd explain what ceiling was, tell him to send us two telegrams a day, and drive on." Mr. Collings is not sure how many trained meteorologists work for Trans World Airlines today—fifty or sixty, he thinks offhand. (Actually there are fifty-six.) But he remembers, precisely, each station he set up on the first airline weather service in the United States—Detroit, Sturgis, Coldwater, White Pigeon, all in Michigan, and Elkhart in Indiana.

Flying on Instruments

Even when weather was learned, there was the problem of what to do about it. That meant instruments. Jack Herlihy, vice president of United Airlines, just last winter committed his company to purchase $200 million worth of jet airliners—planes he discusses with dry mastery of technical detail. But as he talks about instruments, his voice changes, and he is again sitting on his parachute, silk scarf about his neck, peering through his goggles out over the black Alleghenies between Cleveland and Jersey.

"A lot of us were trying to see whether we could get through the clouds, instead of ducking under them and following the canyons," Herlihy recalls. "I put cardboard covers on my goggles with only two slits in them, so I couldn't see anything but the instruments, and forced myself to practice instruments on clear days. Then one day I was flying over a place called Greenwood, Pennsylvania, and I hit this big bump—and instead of looking outside to see what happened, I found I was looking at the instruments first! Then it dawned on me, that this aviation business was going to amount to something . . . but a lot of guys who never learned instruments aren't here today." There are between fifty and sixty instruments on a modern cockpit panel today, and dozens of more subtle ones in development. But the men of Herlihy's day had to prove that airplanes could fly from here to there, through dark skies or cloudy ones, on a single compass, single radio and a simple needle-ball gyroscope to show their tilt and turn. When they had learned that, there were tracks across the sky.

The late twenties were heroic days in aviation. A young man named Lindbergh sped across the Atlantic. America's imagination flared—and the following year applications for pilots' licenses tripled.

On the ground, a solemn young engineer named Herbert Hoover, Jr., began to tinker with radio problems for an outfit that specialized in flying passengers—Western Air Express, later to become part of TWA. Out of his tinkering came a two-way radio for the pilot's cockpit, putting him instantly and permanently in touch with ground control.

Two rival engineering plants, Curtiss-Wright and Pratt & Whitney, began to leapfrog each other, as they have been doing ever since, in providing ever more powerful engines for an industry that clamored always for more power. Out of their rivalry, compact, radial air-cooled motors began to grow to 400 to 600 horsepower to replace the cumbersome leftover designs of World War I. With these new engines, plane makers found new shapes for cabins, wing structures, fuselage.

Yet something continued to be lacking—money and profit. It was only the airmail, an outright subsidy from an indulgent government, that kept the struggling airlines from instant bankruptcy. Profits rested on payment by poundage of mail. Sharp operators could flesh out the dry bones of airmail poundage by trickery—by wrapping heavy telephone books in brown paper and shipping them as airmail over their own lines, or by shipping spare parts and machines, ticketed as airmail, from one field of their operation to another. But there was little or no profit in this.

One could, of course, fly passengers. But passengers, to the early airmen, were a bother—to be jammed on top of the mail-bags up front, or to be kicked off by pilots annoyed by their chatter. Passengers would get sick and foul up the cabins at the bumpy, churning altitudes airplanes then flew. And to fly passengers profitably from, say, New York to San Francisco, would require an air fare of $1,003.12. There was no permanent market to be won at such rates. Today's $80 cost-to-coast tourist fare was, in those days, not even a lunatic's dream. "Fundamentally," says American Airlines' C. R. Smith as he looks back, "we were stuck until we got a new kind of plane, because every passenger seat we sold was sold at a loss."

The financing of the twenties and thirties mirrored this dismal situation; it was based on hope rather than fact, a gamble rather than an investment. The root of airline profits ran to political contacts in Washington, and deals made in Washington back rooms recalled all the squalor of primitive railroad financing eighty years before. Connivance, of course, led to vulnerability—as was proved when the New Deal in its righteous wrath canceled all airmail contracts and nearly wiped out the fledgling industry overnight in the black year 1934. Yet the miracle was about to happen.

C. R. Smith, who only that year had been named president of the rickety agglomeration of routes he was to make into American Airlines, says, "The DC-3 was the miracle. It was the first airplane where, if you sold all the seats, you actually made a little money. I bought the first twenty-five DC-3's when we were so broke we told the Douglas people we'd buy planes only if they didn't ask for a deposit—bought them over the phone, too, and never did sign a contract."

It is good to pause and look at the DC-3, a stubby, silver-winged monoplane, which will someday be enshrined like the Model T Ford and the Conestoga wagon in the museum of America's travel memories. The DC-3, like the great jets of today, was simply a wonderful coming together of innumerable unrecorded triumphs of American imagination in far-flung laboratories and unknown drafting rooms.

The engines, Curtiss-Wright Cyclones, turning up 900 horsepower each, had been born out of Yankee engineering skill just two years earlier, in the sheds of Paterson, New Jersey. On Long Island, another group of engineers at the Sperry plant meshed all the growing family of panel instruments into a master automatic pilot—a device that locked the plane on course and flew it by itself. Along the leading edge of each wing, a boot of rubber flexed slowly back and forth to break the malevolent grip of the ice demon. The DC-3's undercarriage drew up into its body, presenting a smooth surface to the air flow. Uncountable streams of diverse ingenuity had been pulled together by Douglas engineers at Santa Monica to make a plane which flew at altitudes of six thousand to twelve thousand feet and carried six thousand pounds of passenger or payload in twenty-one seats or fourteen berths at 185 miles an hour.

Now, in 1936, aviation's legs began to lengthen. Chicago was a single hop of four hours from New York; the East Coast was three stops, or eighteen hours, from the West Coast. Where formerly money in aviation could be made only from subsidies of government airmail, it could now be made from people, and the horizons were totally new. Only 678,500 Americans had flown the airlines in 1935, the year before the DC-3; five years after the DC-3, this number had almost sextupled. These new passengers wanted neither thrill nor adventure but speed, and they insisted it be backed by safety. These two constants drew the industry faster and faster forward.

As traffic doubled, tripled, multiplied, the air became crowded and demanded traffic control. The way the pilots spin the yarn, traffic control really began in 1935 over Newark, New Jersey, then one of the busiest airports in the country. One day that fall, two pilots sat over coffee in the cafeteria after both had burrowed down to landing through the overcast. "I had the funniest thing happen today," said the first pilot. "I crossed the range at four thousand feet and just as I crossed it I ran into this turbulence, as if the air had rocks in it." "Is that so?" said the second.

"I came in at four thousand, too, and the same thing happened to me when I was on top of the range—I came in at 12:01— what time did you come in?" "Twelve-oh-one," said the first pilot. The two men looked at each other stunned, knowing they had almost grazed wing tips in the thick air just a few minutes earlier.

The Beginning of Traffic Control

It was at Newark, therefore, on December 1, 1935, that four commercial carriers decided to set up a traffic control of their own, with a tower and posting board to make sure that no two of their planes approaching Newark were planning to occupy the same air space at the same moment. In April, 1936, they opened another center at Chicago, in June a third at Cleveland; by July the government, through the Civil Aeronautics Administration, had taken over responsibility for these centers and was opening more. By 1938, eleven different traffic control centers were separating planes by time, by flight levels, by routes all over the country.

Safety and speed were strengthened each month, each year, by a hundred different developments, meeting and marrying each other in the unique and unpredictable romance of American technology. Thus, in 1937, TWA, seeking a way to fly higher, fitted out an experimental Northrop at its Kansas City base with a whirling, compressive device called a "supercharger." The "supercharger" was ready because engineers and metallurgists had for years been working at General Electric on metals that could withstand high temperatures and centrifugal forces, and had only just solved the problem. The supercharger made it possible for airplane engines to thrive on the rarefied air of the upper atmosphere. This in turn freed the airframe of the plane from the thick, dragging lower atmosphere and allowed it to slice through the quick, clean air of the stratosphere. But to use this height the entire plane had to be redesigned. It had to be pressurized, to give passengers enough oxygen to breathe safely.

By 1940, Boeing had produced a pressurized Stratoliner, flying at 220 miles an hour; it was not only quicker, cheaper and faster, but infinitely safer, because it could cruise at eighteen thousand to twenty thousand feet, high above the grasping fingers of the Rockies. The airmen could look down now on Utah's ominous Wasatch Range, where the bones of aviation pioneers whitened, and the Wasatch was no longer there to haunt them, as the Alleghenies were no longer there when the DC-3 blew in.

All the while men of the domestic airlines were mastering the heights of continental America, other men were attempting to master the sweep of the oceans. They were operating under the flag of a single company, Pan American, lavishly supported by the United States government. Pan American had first spread its wings over the Gulf of Mexico, flying thirsty citizens from the parched deserts of Prohibition America to the oases of Havana's bars. Between 1927 and 1934, it stretched its span to the farthest tip of South America. By the spring of 1935 its expeditionary ship, the North Haven, a black Japanese-built freighter, was laying bases on unknown islands of the Pacific. By November of that year, with a radio communication system all across the Pacific and island bases at every stop, with the new Martin 130 Flying Boat ready for action, the China Clipper could take the air from Alameda Bay, California, and report arrival in Manila in three and a half days (fifty-nine hours, fifty minutes of flying time later). By May of 1939 it was the Atlantic's turn, when the first Clipper out of New York made its landfall in Lisbon. But by then the war was on its way—and the war was to make of domestic and overseas airlines one community of the air and whirl them both forward on their way.

In aviation the war was an incubating force. Across the Atlantic, the British and American governments flung a magic labyrinth of electronic aids as the pilots of every airline, as well as thousands of civilians in uniform, learned the art of ocean navigation. From the seedbed of engineering dreams new engines, shapes, planes were wrung faster and faster. The great four-engined prototypes of the postwar era—Douglas's DC-4 and Lockheed's Constellation—first made their bow in war paint, as by the thousands they infected Americans with their war-born contempt for distance.

At home, the war ripped airports and towers from the control of individual cities and private companies and gave the Civil Aeronautics Administration direct radio contact and control over all planes from takeoff to landing. The crush of emergency traffic forced uniform new procedures. By 1945 these new procedures and new devices were bringing planes in to land by instruments at the rate of twelve an hour, in any weather, with far greater safety than in 1941 when only four an hour could be handled.

Yet the war did more than incubate air technology; it incubated Americans' demand for air travel. The first postwar year of flying, 1946, saw more than four times as many passengers aloft as flew in 1940, America's last prewar year. Under the hammering of new nonscheduled airlines (mostly bands of ex-servicemen with engineering or flying experience), fares began to drop to their present coach-fare low of $80 coast to coast. And as fares dropped, as prosperous America's leisure and wanderlust soared, air traffic surged in a tide that shows no sign of slackening.

The years since the war have not been quiet years in aviation. Yet they have been waiting years, a long pause before a bigger question mark. On every frontier, aviation's advance has continued—but it has been advance on marked paths, whose signposts have long been known.

The weather has been learned, and weathermen plot plane courses over continent and ocean to fly the pressure pattern of the winds, flipping from tail wind to tail wind in a manner that mocks yesterday's obsolete mile measurements. One day the winds may make the shortest distance between New York and Los Angeles lie across Canada, the next day across the Gulf of Mexico, the next, directly over the middle of the country.

Instrumentation has been elaborated both on the field and in the cockpit.

The new master planes of the postwar years, the Douglas DC-7 and Lockheed Super-Constellation, have stretched the legs of aviation until both continent and ocean are a single jump. American planes, American procedures, Americanese itself, have become the code of all flying everywhere. "You come down out of the night," said a Pan Am pilot in reflective wonder, "and there's Istanbul below—talking English from the tower." As first TWA, then Delta, then Northwest, then Braniff followed Pan American to foreign shores, in the postwar years competition has pushed American standards ever higher. Today American overseas navigation and efficiency have become as much the standard of intercontinental air as the operation of the white-sailed American clippers was the standard on the broad seas a century ago.

Essentially, however, nothing either radical or new has happened in the aviation industry from 1948 until the year just past [1955, when jet planes were first manufactured in the United States for commercial use].

The engineers who like to philosophize about technology find this natural. As their art developed a generation ago, they point out, the easy first steps followed one another, almost month by month. But each further new step became more complicated, more costly, more difficult.

Each major new achievement thus became a plateau of development measurably longer in time than the one before. The DC-3 was master of the commercial skies for ten years. By 1959 the postwar, four-engined, pressurized planes will have reigned for fourteen years. Each has required time, first to teach its operators the problems, then to teach the community its opportunity.

Now comes the jet, and the jet plateau promises to be the longest yet. The jet finally ends speed competition among planes. Flying at 550 to 600 miles an hour, it slams the plane's nose right up against the sound barrier.

Whatever plane eventually succeeds the jet will have to be able to jab a full planeload of civilian-suited passengers all the way *through* the sound barrier right up to the heat barrier—with speeds twice those considered practical today. This, say the engineers, will be a long, long day in coming. The jet is thus the plane of our immediate future, with a life reign of fifteen to twenty years. In this period we must learn to solve the problems the jet raises before we can begin to worry [about] the problems of the plateau beyond it.

THE CIVIL AERONAUTICS BOARD AND THE CIVIL AERONAUTICS ADMINISTRATION [2]

In 1926 the Aeronautics Branch was formed as a part of the United States Department of Commerce, charged with the licensing of pilots, making flying safe, developing new air navigation facilities, mapping the airways, and furnishing flight information. The Branch was established under the Air Commerce Act, the first Federal legislation for aviation. In 1934 its name was changed to the Bureau of Air Commerce.

The Civil Aeronautics Act of 1938 created a successor, the Civil Aeronautics Authority. This Authority consisted of an Administrator and a quasi-judicial board of five members, all appointed by the President. It inherited the personnel and duties of the Bureau of Air Commerce and certain duties of the Post Office Department and the Interstate Commerce Commission.

In the summer of 1940, the Civil Aeronautics Authority underwent two reorganizations to attain its present form. Actually, the Authority now exists only on paper. It is more accurate to refer to its two separately functioning parts, the Civil Aeronautics Administration and the Civil Aeronautics Board, the latter consisting of a five-man panel. The Board is an independent, quasi-judicial organization; the Administration is an executive agency under the Department of Commerce.

[In general, the Board performs three chief functions: (1) regulation of the economic aspects of domestic and international United States air carrier operations; (2) promulgation of safety standards and Civil Air Regulations; (3) investigation and analysis of civil aircraft accidents.

Economic Regulation. The Board authorizes domestic and international United States air carrier service and grants permits to foreign air carriers serving the United States. The Board exercises regulatory powers over United States air carriers in the filing of tariffs, it regulates and prescribes rates for the carriage of persons and property, establishes rates of compensation for the carriage of mail, and regulates accounts, records and reports,

[2] From *The CAA Story*, pamphlet. United States Department of Commerce. Civil Aeronautics Administration. Washington 25, D.C. 1957.

mergers, loans and financial aid, methods of competition, and interlocking relationships. With the advice and assistance of the Secretary of State, the Board participates in the negotiation of agreements with foreign governments for the establishment and development of air routes and services.

Safety Regulation. The Board prescribes safety standards, rules and regulations, and has the power to suspend and revoke safety certificates after hearing. The Board also acts on complaints filed by the Civil Aeronautics Administration of the Department of Commerce with respect to violations of the United States Civil Air Regulations and has the power to revoke and suspend United States civil airman certificates.

Accident Investigation and Analysis. The Board investigates accidents involving civil aircraft and holds public hearings to assist in determining the facts, circumstances and probable causes; it makes such recommendations to the Administrator as will tend to prevent similar accidents in the future; makes such reports and recommendations public as may be deemed by it to be in the public interest; and conducts special studies and investigations to reduce aircraft accidents and prevent their recurrence.—Ed.]

The Civil Aeronautics Administration is a Bureau of the United States Department of Commerce and is headed by an Administrator who is appointed by the President. . . . It has six program offices: Office of Air Traffic Control, Office of Air Navigation Facilities, Office of Flight Operations and Airworthiness, Office of Airports, Office of International Cooperation, and the Technical Development Center in Indianapolis, Indiana.

In addition to the program offices of CAA, there are several staff offices, the Aeronautical Center, and six regional offices. Each regional office is headed by a Regional Administrator and has divisions which parallel the Washington offices, such as Airports Division, Air Navigation Facilities Division, and Air Carrier Safety Division.

Air Traffic Control and Air Navigation Facilities. Control of the nation's air traffic is the responsibility of the CAA. Building and maintaining the air navigation facilities and controlling air traffic was formerly the responsibility of the CAA Office of Federal Airways. Because of the vast growth of air traffic the functions have now been divided. The Office of Air Traffic Control operates CAA's air traffic control facilities—air route traffic control centers, airport traffic control towers, and communications stations—which are designed to maintain the safe and orderly separation of aircraft along the Federal airways and at airports and to furnish weather and other aeronautical data to pilots. The Office of Air Navigation Facilities is responsible for the design, construction, maintenance, and inspection of navigation, traffic control, and communications equipment for the airways.

CAA has been . . . controlling air traffic since July 6, 1936. The original group of controllers numbered only ten, located at Newark, Chicago, and Cleveland. Now, twenty years later, in the continental United States alone CAA employs more than 9,500 persons performing air traffic control duties at 500 locations and more than 3,000 maintenance specialists keeping over 91,000 miles of airways operating without interruption twenty-four hours a day.

The extent of the present control job is illustrated by the traffic figures for 1956, when there were approximately 22 million landings and takeoffs at airports having CAA traffic control towers and over 25 million fix postings. Fix postings are reports of en route aircraft over compulsory check points along the airways.

What is air traffic control and how is it accomplished? Air traffic control is nothing more nor less than providing aircraft in flight with longitudinal, lateral, or vertical separation from other aircraft. Complicating factors which enter the control picture include weather, geography, operating characteristics of many different types of aircraft, human elements affecting pilots and controllers, amount of traffic, and many other factors.

The nation's air traffic moves under two sets of rules: Visual Flight Rules (VFR), which is normal in good weather when the rules are "see and be seen;" and Instrument Flight Rules (IFR), which are required when the weather is bad and visibility is restricted. From an en route traffic control standpoint, the CAA is concerned exclusively with IFR traffic. It has virtually no control over VFR operations except in the immediate vicinity of airports.

To control the traffic along the airways and at busy terminal points, the CAA has divided the country geographically into twenty-six segments. In each has been established a control facility known as an Air Route Traffic Control Center (ARTC). These twenty-six Centers carry the full authority for the control of all air traffic operating under IFR conditions. In practice, the Centers control en route traffic between terminal points; they delegate to CAA airport traffic control towers the control over traffic operating in a radius of approximately twenty miles around an airport.

A third type of facility in the control system is the Air Traffic Communications Station (ATCS), which may be separately located or combined with tower or center. While direct control decisions are not made at ATCS facilities, these stations play an important role in the over-all traffic control picture. They form the communications link between controllers and pilots in flight along the airways, they provide pre-flight and in-flight briefing, and they are available for flight advisory service among other essential duties.

These three types of facilities—the centers, the towers and the communications stations—are linked by 115,933 miles of teletype and 121,714 miles of interphone lines so that they can work in close coordination with each other. . . .

In 1926, when the operation of the Federal Airways System began, 2,041 miles of airways were in operation. The revolving light beacon was the principal guide to early pilots—largely those flying the airmail—in their cross-country flights at night. . . .

The 1930's brought the low- or medium-frequency four-course radio range (L/MF) to guide the pilot along the airways, and it became the principal navigational aid. The rapid growth in aviation after the war, with the great increase in aircraft speed, made a more reliable system imperative. The answer was found in very high frequency omnidirectional radio ranges (VOR). More than 91,000 miles of airways in the United States now are served by 445 VOR installations.

CAA will implement the airways system with an estimated 1,200 VORTAC installations. VORTAC is a combination of VOR and TACAN (tactical air navigation). TACAN is a military development. When combined under one roof, the VORTAC equipment provides two sources of bearing information, one from the VOR and one from the TACAN, and one source of distance measuring information from the TACAN.

Other en route aids are radio beacons and fan markers, which mark airway intersections and are used as reporting points.

Radar is becoming an increasingly important tool in controlling traffic. New long-range radar ordered in 1956 will have a range of 150 miles. Already operating are airport surveillance radar (ASR), which has a range of thirty miles and shows aircraft flying within the terminal area, and precision approach radar (PAR) for monitoring or "talk-down" of pilots on final approach. There are now thirty-seven ASR's and ten PAR's in use in the continental United States.

For actual landings under IFR conditions a pilot has a choice of an Instrument Landing System (ILS) let-down, where a radio "beam" activates a cockpit instrument that shows him whether to fly left, right, up, or down; of being "talked down" by a controller using PAR; or of using both methods.

Visual aids to approach for landing include high intensity lighting of the approach path and lighting systems on the runway.

Using radar in approach control and in departure control, controllers can handle as many aircraft under IFR conditions as they can under VFR conditions.

With the steady increase in air traffic, certain limitations have become apparent in the current control system. The main approach to a solution of the problem is through radar, with the goal of eventual complete radar coverage of the airspace at higher altitudes. Corollary needs are: Direct communications between the controller and all pilots within range of his radar; and a more extensive, more exact system of navigation aids which will enable a pilot to hold an assigned course without heavy reliance on ground instructions. Other deficiencies call for intensive research and development work. [See "Safety in the

Air" in this section below.] Meanwhile, CAA adheres to its policy of maintaining safety by limiting its acceptance of traffic to the capacity of the control system while doing its best to increase that capacity.

Office of Flight Operations and Airworthiness. Safety in aviation is a basic responsibility of the entire CAA; but the specific job of certificating aircraft and airmen is assigned to the Office of Flight Operations and Airworthiness.

Its aeronautical inspectors watch over the progress of a new aircraft from the time it is designed until it is in the customer's hands for operation. To start, aeronautical engineers prepare standards for use by manufacturers in producing safe planes. When a plane is produced as a prototype and is successfully flight tested and approved by CAA, it receives a type certificate and the manufacturer may turn it out in numbers.

CAA's certification workload is now at an all-time high. There are twenty-five turbine-powered aircraft before it for approval during the next three years. Of this new type of aircraft, eleven are of foreign manufacture. In addition, there are nine helicopters and sixteen new smaller planes in the group to be checked by CAA experts in airframes, power plant, and flight testing before CAA certification is given. There are also new accessories of all kinds which must be CAA approved before manufacturers can sell planes equipped with them.

The mechanics who keep planes airworthy, the pilots who fly them, and (in the case of air carriers) the navigators, radio operators, and engineers aboard and the dispatchers who send the planes on their journeys, all must qualify under CAA rules for their competency, and earn certificates.

The CAA also approves schools that teach flying and train mechanics, and sets standards for these schools which insure proper training. It publishes study material for use in preparing for the examinations required for the airmen certificates.

The CAA requires regular inspection of aircraft to insure their airworthiness and provides aircraft owners with current information on proper maintenance and special care of their planes. It also keeps records on aircraft ownership and airmen certificates.

CAA develops and recommends medical standards which airmen must meet and carries on aviation medical research at CAA's Medical Research Laboratory at Ohio State University, Columbus.

CAA maintains three types of Flight Operations and Airworthiness District Offices throughout the country, each serving a specific area and operating under the direction of one of the six regional offices.

The most numerous of these district offices are those which serve the public in general aviation matters. Inspectors stationed in these offices travel a regular itinerary of airports in their district to conduct examinations for airmen and other general aviation business.

The inspectors at the air carrier district offices are experts in maintenance, operation, or communications. They work with the airlines in establishing systems designed to achieve a high level of safety in these fields, then spot check the operation of the systems. You may see a CAA inspector on any airline trip you take, though he will be hard to identify. His work is with the crew and he may be sitting on the "jump" seat between the pilots, observing their conduct of the flight; or he may be sitting alongside the navigator or flight engineer "up front." This work by the CAA, together with the airlines' own deep concern for safety, year after year has produced better safety records for United States air carriers. In 1956, for example [despite the crash of two airliners over the Grand Canyon that took 125 lives] there were 0.6 passenger fatalities for every 100 million passenger miles flown by the domestic scheduled airlines and no passenger fatalities in either international scheduled or irregular air carrier operations.

The Aircraft Engineering District Office is the headquarters for CAA's manufacturing inspectors. These inspectors make a continuing inspection of the aircraft being manufactured and of the manufacturer's quality control procedures and processes.

On January 1, 1954, the Civil Aeronautics Board delegated to the Civil Aeronautics Administration the investigation of accidents involving fixed-wing aircraft of 12,500 pounds or under. This type of accident investigation is the responsibility of the Office of Flight Operations and Airworthiness. The CAB retained responsibility for accidents to fixed-wing aircraft of over 12,500 pounds, aircraft used in Alaskan air carrier operations regardless of weight, and helicopters or other non-fixed-wing aircraft.

Office of Airports. The principal job of the Office of Airports is the planning, development, and perpetuation of an adequate national system of airports.

A major part of this work is done with the Federal Aid Airport Program, through which the CAA allots money to local airport sponsors usually on a fifty-fifty matching basis, to produce such an adequate system.

The Office of Airports assists communities in the layout, design, and construction of airports and airport facilities, always with the aim of handling existing and expected air traffic in that locality. It establishes standards which must be followed on projects sharing Federal funds and which it recommends in all other cases. Publications such as *Airport Design, Airport Paving, Airport Terminal Building,* and *Small Airports* are prepared to assist communities and advance these standards.

Under the Federal Aid Airport Program, which was established in 1946 by an Act of Congress, the CAA had allocated $326,569,000 in Federal funds to localities to assist with 3,410 projects at 1,385 airports through May 31, 1957. Under this program, the CAA can assist with land purchase, with the construction of most buildings except hangars, and with lighting, paving, and all the facilities that contribute to the safe use of an airport.

The CAA does not license airports nor assist and advise in their fiscal operation.

Office of International Cooperation. In the international field, the CAA is concerned with many of the problems it faces domestically. Safety and airways specialists are stationed in the eleven International Field Offices at Bangkok, Beirut, Buenos Aires, Frankfort, Lima, London, Manila, Paris, Rio de Janeiro, San Juan, and Tokyo. They carry on their usual services for United States air commerce in their areas, and for the foreign airlines which fly from there to the United States. These CAA men are often called upon by foreign governments to serve as aviation advisers and consultants.

The CAA sends technical assistance missions to various countries on specific aviation problems. Upward of thirty missions are in the field at one time, assisting in such matters as airways aids for India, a multimillion dollar system of airports for Colombia, training air traffic controllers for Japan, or a new and modern flight information center for Latin American nations.

The International Cooperation Administration provides funds to the CAA as a part of United States technical assistance to friendly nations. The over-all purpose of the CAA is to produce standard airways throughout the world, with aids and procedures uniform everywhere as a major contribution to air travel safety. Hundreds of foreign nationals are brought here by ICA for specialized training, and scores of high officials from other countries have come here to observe and study United States methods, facilities and procedures under CAA arrangements.

Technical Development Center. The CAA maintains a Technical Development Center in Indianapolis, Indiana, where ideas and inventions valuable in aviation are evaluated and developed for practical use. . . . Studies often are conducted with the cooperation of the aviation industry and the military services.

[On August 23, 1958, President Eisenhower signed into law a measure creating a Federal Aviation Agency that will take over all the duties and responsibilities of the Civil Aeronautics Authority described above and will replace it. The FAA, which will be an independent agency, will also assume the Civil Aeronautics Board's function of writing air safety regulations, leaving to the CAB all its other functions (including the investigation of air accidents and the determination of airline routes and subsidies) listed at the beginning of this article. The broad role of the new agency, as described by law, will be to regulate and promote civil aviation and "to provide for safe and efficient use of the air space by both civil and military aircraft." Long needed and desired by all segments of aviation, the FAA will assume and coordinate powers over the industry now spread haphazardly throughout some forty government agencies and departments. In a recess appointment on September 30, President Eisenhower named Elwood R. Quesada as administrator of the FAA, the appointment to take effect November 1. The agency is to begin functioning February 1, 1959.—Ed.]

DC MEANS DOUGLAS COMMERCIAL [3]

To leaders of one of the great industries in the United States, aircraft manufacturing, a man named Donald Douglas has become a living legend. To the general public he remains a shadowy figure, rarely photographed, even more rarely interviewed. Yet this unobtrusive citizen is perhaps more responsible than any other man alive for America's unquestioned leadership in commercial aviation. The chances are better than even that any airliner you ride will bear the hallmark DC—Douglas Commercial. Today Douglas plants have turned out over 52 per cent of the free world's airliners, more than all other companies put together.

Young Donald Douglas himself hardly foresaw this in 1920 when, with a wife, two children, a dog, a bucket-seat jalopy and $600 in savings, he drove into Los Angeles, determined to set up an airplane business for himself. This had been his dream since a boyhood day when he had thrilled to the sight of a "flying machine" wobbling incredibly through the air. He was now twenty-eight and had graduated from Massachusetts Institute of Technology, had served as technical adviser to the United States Signal Corps during World War I, had worked for a short time for Glenn Martin, designing the Martin bomber, first plane to sink a battleship.

In Los Angeles Douglas rented desk space back of a barbershop. To feed his family, the husky engineer hired out as a laborer, hoed potatoes, washed cars. The frugality which still characterizes him has roots in this precarious period.

The miracle happened when a friend, newsman Bill Henry, steered a $40,000 airplane order to the barbershop. The custo-

[3] From "The Man Who Wrote DC in the Sky," article by Francis Drake, author of *Vertical Warfare*, and Katharine Drake, former dramatic editor of the New York *World-Telegram*. *Reader's Digest*. 72:134-5+. March 1958. Copyright 1958 by The Reader's Digest Association, Inc. Reprinted with permission.

mer, wealthy sportsman David R. Davis, wanted to hang up a new record—coast-to-coast nonstop. In those days planes existed mainly to capture "firsts," and the assumption was that Douglas would come up with a high-powered, gas-guzzling, one-shot headline hunter. But the young designer chose this moment to break out the uncompromising standard which still flies from his mast. Aircraft design, he insisted, should be cumulative—the plane of today should incorporate seed for the plane of tomorrow. All Douglas planes, military or commercial, have been built in series. The DC's represent a process of evolution as controlled as generations of prize cattle bred from successively better stock.

Soon a remarkable plane was taking shape on Douglas's drawing board. Named the *Cloudster,* it was built by hand in a loft, with tools rented from a piano factory downstairs. Assisting Douglas were just six young men (whose wives stitched the fabric to the wings). An engine mishap cost Davis the record, but the *Cloudster* hung up a "first" of greater consequence: It was the first plane to lift its weight in payload.

The *Cloudster* became popular with the military overnight. In 1921 the Navy ordered three planes, adapted to torpedo carrying. Then the Army turned the international spotlight on the modest Douglas plant that had arisen in a Santa Monica field. In three single-engine amphibious biplanes designed by Douglas, the Army pulled off the first aerial circumnavigation of the globe. With navigational aids consisting of a compass and some prewar maps (cockpit radio was still undreamed of), the planes took off over the North Pacific on April 6, 1924. They buffeted their way across twenty-two countries, 27,553 miles. Under conditions inconceivable to modern pilots, they landed catch-as-catch-can in snowdrifts, equatorial swamps, rice paddies, opening up routes that form the skeleton of today's global operations. Fifty thousand jubilant citizens of Santa Monica, carpeting two acres of runway with fresh roses, acclaimed their safe return.

At this point Douglas's life was one long scramble after working capital. Government orders streamed in, but how to finance construction? The government did not pay until planes were tested and delivered. More than anything, what hampered Douglas's business deals was his exceptionally boyish face, which stamped him as a generation younger than his years. He was in his thirties, father of four sons and a daughter, but many still mistook him for an undergraduate. To prepare for his first attempt to borrow money ($35,000) from a bank, he grew a mustache, hoping to look more worldly. The loan was granted but, at parting, the banker said: "Shave it off, kid—you're not fooling anybody!" Douglas has remained clean-shaven ever since. . . .

Military business helped, but it did not fulfill the Douglas dream, which was to get an earthbound traveling public into the skies. Pioneer airlines had begun precarious daylight operations, but they managed to exist largely through government mail subsidies. Opportunity came in 1932, when Jack Frye, then vice president of Trans-Continental and Western Airlines (now TWA), asked Douglas for an airliner that would really attract passengers and enable his line to operate in the black, independent of subsidies.

Characteristically, before accepting the challenge Douglas dispatched an assistant engineer as an observer on a routine transcontinental flight. Ten days went by before the young man reappeared—by train—still pale from his ordeal and slightly deaf. He summed up the 1932 airliner situation as follows: the coast-to-coast "express," making twelve stops to refuel, had battered its way east through a succession of storms, powerless to fly above them, and unable, because of mail commitments, to sit them out. For thirty flying-hours passengers had been rocked, rolled, pitched and tossed. The cabin wasn't soundproofed; all aboard were reduced to lip-reading routines. Moreover, it had reeked of gas, and smoking was not permitted. Throughout the long trip there had been nothing hot to eat or drink.

Douglas lost no time. His initial effort, the DC-1, on its test flight, staggered beholders by flying fully loaded from Winslow, Arizona, to Albuquerque, New Mexico, on a single engine. An improved version, the DC-2, went into production. Orders poured in, but Douglas, still dissatisfied, produced only 130 of these planes. He now took what proved to be a historic stride—production of the twenty-one-passenger DC-3.

The DC-3 became the best known, most beloved transport plane ever built. Phenomenally strong, it boasted reclining seats, soundproofing, air conditioning, hot and cold-water, a galley, night-flying equipment, an automatic pilot, duplicate instrument panels. It slashed coast-to-coast travel time in half, inspired a rush for airline ticket offices. By 1939 the DC-3 had latched onto 90 per cent of the world's airline business. In almost twenty-five years of operation, not one has ever been know to wear out (some have outlived as many as sixty engine changes). Today, more than five thousand DC-3's are still in daily service, including the military version, C-47. . . .

But it was during World War II that the DC-3 achieved classic stature. She evacuated wounded by the tens of thousands, transported jeeps, bulldozers, supplies, ammunition, USO entertainers and mail from home. Countless GI's remember riding her bucket seats through tropical storms, wing tips whipping up and down, static fire playing around the leading edges, engines surging with each sledge-hammer bump. Unarmed but fearless, Old Faithful shuttled supplies across the dangerous Hump in volume surpassing that carried by the Burma Road, was cited by General Eisenhower as "one of the four major weapons of the war." Rammed by kamikazes, riddled by ack-ack, divorced from tail, rudder, ailerons, wing sections, landing gear, nine times out of ten she staggered back to base. . . .

Most significant of Douglas's contributions, however, was his remodeling of overseas transportation. Before the war, convinced that flying-boats had outlived their usefulness, that land-based planes on *wheels* could handle overwater operations with more efficiency and less danger, he had begun work on a four-engine, long-distance version of the DC-3. Titled the DC-4, it was destined to become the forerunner of all of today's ocean-going planes.

But following Pearl Harbor a telegram from the War Department abruptly ordered him to drop the project. Appalled by such unrealistic thinking, Douglas urged on the Secretary of War the critical importance of large transports which could over-leap enemy submarines and quickly reach the remotest battle front.

Rebuffed, Douglas nevertheless continued to produce the new planes.

Three months later a second telegram reversed the first and the DC-4 (Air Force title: C-54) moved into battle as the workhorse of the war. Laden with soldiers and equipment, it made nearly 100,000 ocean crossings. It enabled President Roosevelt, Winston Churchill, General Eisenhower and other Allied leaders to meet frequently, with the minimum of danger and delay. It climaxed its performance by carrying General Douglas MacArthur and two divisions of troops to Tokyo to accept the Japanese surrender, and later by powering the Berlin Airlift almost single-handed. . . .

Douglas believes the worst crisis he ever faced was the one brought him by a Western Union boy on V-J Day. The telegram canceled all government orders as of that instant. All the cash in the till could not have carried the payroll more than a month. His war profits had amounted to no more than one half of one per cent of sales. In one black week Douglas had to lay off ninety thousand men and women. His whole carefully created structure, the complex plants, precision tools, the highly skilled employees and technical teams faced disintegration. Douglas finally hit upon a plan that promised help.

He took a decision of extraordinary boldness, since it involved risking most of the company's remaining assets. He decided to produce a radically different passenger plane, one which could operate *at high altitude,* where thinner air would make for faster speeds and more economical operation.

Between the vision and the achievement lay supreme engineering difficulties. Still to be perfected were (1) a cabin able to withstand tons of inside pressure; (2) superchargers to pump outside air (often 100 degrees below zero) into the cabin at 70 degrees above; (3) insulation light enough to be economical, impenetrable enough to withstand tremendous cold; (4) double-paned windows, impervious to blowout; (5) "anti-icing boots," foolproof against increased icing hazards.

After an earlier experimental DC-5 has been discarded, the first high-flying three-hundred-mile-per-hour DC-6's, carrying sixty passengers, began operation in 1947. By 1953, four hundred of them were aloft, serving twenty-seven airlines. That year Douglas followed up with the DC-7's. Long, slim, shimmering, able to carry eighty passengers at great altitude in unprecedented luxury, they inaugurated the first nonstop coast-to-coast service.

Douglas is the only major aircraft producer to have rounded out the whole spectacular cycle of aviation from the earliest propeller-driven planes to the latest jets. Last year the Douglas fleets logged over 82 million of the 160 million passenger miles flown each day throughout the world, and the company's five plants, so vast that office messengers wear roller skates, turned out more than one billion dollars' worth of military and commercial aircraft and missiles.

Today Douglas is concentrating on the DC-8, the 150-passenger, 150-ton, all-jet airliner. . . . The red-hot race to capture the jet market marks one time when a DC entry was not present at the starting gun. Douglas held back in 1952 when the British Comets stole the first march. Later, when the French Caravelle invaded the skies, he let his most formidable rival, Boeing, get a head start. (Boeing, which had long experience in building high-altitude jet bombers for the Air Force, used this experience to produce a passenger prototype, the 707, which [in April 1957] flew from Seattle to Baltimore in three hours, forty-seven minutes. The 707 will be in service almost a year ahead of the DC-8.)

The reasons for his deliberation at that time are twofold, says Douglas. First, in the early fifties the airlines had about $1.5 billion tied up in propeller planes, many of them brand new. To have brought out jet transports at this point would have involved the industry in tremendous refinancing difficulties. Second, the terrible fate that overtook the pioneering Comets drew attention to many specialized problems, including metal fatigue. Douglas refused to commit himself to the manufacture of jet transports until he had perfected a cabin strong enough to hold a pressure twice that of the DC-6 and subjected it to 300,000 simulated climbs and descents of the kind that had wrecked the Comets. After tests that simulated one hundred years of flying, he finally tooled up for DC-8 production.

By the time the first DC-8 takes to the air the Douglas Company's investment in the plane will be more than $200 million, all of which could go down the drain if flight tests should fail to come up to expectation. So great, however, is the industry's faith in the DC planes that fourteen of the world's airlines have placed orders for 133 of them, at $5.5 million apiece.

The DC-8 will feature cocktail lounges, with divans and bridge tables, tape-recorded music, shaded lights, outsized berths. Like Boeing's 707, it will also offer one of the least fatiguing rides in transportation history, noiseless, vibrationless. It will have an effect on schedules so bewildering that few have yet grasped the oncoming shrinkage of our world. A passenger will be able to week-end in Europe, leaving New York on Friday night and taking early breakfast in Paris six hours later. On Sunday evening he will leave at 10 P.M. and, because of the difference in time, land in New York at 11:30 P.M.

With the DC-8 nearing completion, Douglas is still covering sheets of paper with symbols and equations. Up in one corner there invariably appears a neat engineer's sketch of a long, slim object. Its futuristic look suggests supersonic adventures. The mathematics keep resolving back into the same brackets—one thousand to fifteen hundred miles per hour. Is this the first glimmer of the DC-9? Donald Douglas is not admitting it. But if it is, it will be worth waiting for. . . .

"CONSTELLATIONS" IN THE SKY [4]

In Burbank, California, one day [in 1946] a big shark-bodied plane rose from the Lockheed Air Terminal, circled out across the San Fernando Valley and headed east over the mountains. It was a notable event and a red-letter day for Pan American Airways: that was the first of the fleet of Lockheed Constellations for Pan Am's globe-girdling routes.

To the Lockheed Aircraft Corporation, it was an event, too. But in the sprawling cluster of factory buildings, still in their muddy green and yellow camouflage of war, everyone was too busy to cheer. On the long assembly lines, workers were hustling at wartime pace to turn out Constellations for others of the world's demanding airlines. . . .

[4] From "Salesman at Work." *Time*. 47:77-86. January 14, 1946. This article is reprinted by permission from *Time* Magazine; copyright Time Inc. 1946.

What spurred them all was "Connie's" proved performance —a much-improved performance over any existing airliner's. . . . Airlines which didn't have Constellations feared that travelers would ride on airlines which did. Lockheed's sleek new beauties had quietly started a postwar revolution in air travel. . . .

The new constellation in the firmament was the result of another astronomical phenomenon: the shooting-star career of the Lockheed Corporation itself. Thirteen years ago [1933] the company was sold for $40,000. Now [1946] it had nearly $50 million in working capital. Then, it had only fifteen employees. Now it has 32,000. The end of the war, which had sent most big planemakers into reconversion on a lower key, had not knocked it off its high bracket. Its backlog of orders for planes was perhaps the greatest in the aircraft industry, a thumping $215 million.

Some of this was due to the fortunes of war: like other planemakers, Lockheed had grown big on war orders. The difference was that when war building ended, Lockheed was better prepared for peace than any other company. Both Lockheed's rise and its ability to keep its altitude after war's end were devoutly attributed by Lockheed men to the eccentric talents of their president, Robert Ellsworth Gross.

Bob Gross . . . is a small . . . well-built man with a pink face, greying brown hair and bright blue eyes. Among planemaking tycoons, predominantly an inbred and individualistic group of onetime designers and pilots, Bob Gross is a sport. He is not a pilot. He knows little about aerodynamics. As a production man and administrator he is just so-so. Yet he has one talent which more than balances these apparent deficiencies.

He has a seemingly intuitive salesman's sense of knowing what planes will be wanted a few years hence [see "Freight and the Future" in Section II, below] and then being ready to deliver them. On top of this, he has the knack of getting his ideas across, and a flair for picking men who can translate them into planes.

As a diligent collector of modern art, Bob Gross has developed an artistic sense which sometimes enables him to feel something wrong in a plane simply because it is esthetically unpleasant. He feels that a plane which does not look right won't fly right.

Free of the inhibitions that aerodynamic knowledge might give, he has a mystical faith in the future of aviation. He is full of such Buck Rogerish ideas as his Flying Man: "Before long we'll have people flying through the air with little motors attached to their backs controlled from a central power source. It's a damn good idea, you know.". . .

A faintly flat "a" still marks Bob Gross as a Bostonian. His family was fairly well-to-do, but his mother, of whom he says he is still scared to death, disapproved of the local schools. So she tutored Bob at home until he was ten. Then she put him in the first grade at public school. She had taught him so well that by afternoon he had been promoted to fifth grade. He spent his last school year at fashionable St. George's School in Newport. At Harvard he turned into a joiner and a doer. . . . After graduation, with only average grades, he put in a short tour of duty in the . . . [post-World War I] army. Then his father's friend George Lee gave him a job in his investment banking house of Lee, Higginson and Company.

Bob Gross learned about the stock market so fast that he was soon making money in it. He also bought and sold small companies. Before he was thirty, he had made $1 million. With some of his cash he decided to go into the aviation business. It was not a whim: he had faith in its money-making future. He formed the Viking Flying Boat Company to build sport-model seaplanes. The depression wiped out the market for seaplanes, along with most of Gross's million. He went to the West Coast to work for an airline. Gross was mightily impressed by the line's fast, sleek plywood Orions. They were made by Lockheed, which had been started in 1916 by two barnstorming brothers, Allan and Malcolm Loughead (pronounced Lockheed). Their planes were already famed; Wiley Post had circled the globe in a Vega, Sir Hubert Wilkins flew one over the Arctic Circle to Spitzbergen, the Lindberghs flew a later model, the Sirius, "north to the Orient." But Lockheed's till was empty. In the great pre-depression merger mania, the Loughead brothers sold out to the Detroit Aircraft Corporation. Detroit Aircraft soon went broke.

One day Bob Gross got a phone call. The caller introduced himself as Carl Squier, general manager of the Lockheed Aircraft Company. Gross had never met him, but Squier, a crack salesman who made it his business to know people, had heard of Gross. Over the phone, Squier sold Gross the idea of forming a syndicate to buy the moribund Lockheed Company. He did, and they did—for $40,000. [The company's founder, Allan Loughead, considered bidding for his old company. But he could raise only $50,000 and thought any bid that low would be an insult. While he was still trying to raise $100,000, Gross bought the company.] Bob Gross and gregarious, sport-jacketed Carl Squier began operations with fifteen employees and only $800 in the bank.

Gross knew what the trouble had been with Lockheed. It had been making planes for the small private-plane market, instead of for the big airlines. Lockheed could not hope to buck Donald Douglas [see "DC Means Douglas Commercial," above] whose DC-2 dominated the two-engined field. The only hope seemed to be in the small transport field. Gross decided to gamble. He spent $139,400 on the Electra, a ten-passenger, all-metal plane for small airlines. The gamble paid off. Gross sold forty of them the next year and put Lockheed into the black. Lockheed then tried a bigger plane, Model 14. It sold, too, and Howard Hughes dramatized the plane to the world by flying one around the globe for a new record: ninety-one hours, seventeen minutes.

When war was near salesman Gross sent brother Courtlandt [Courtlandt Sherrington Gross, vice president and general manager] to London to sell Lockheeds to the British. The answer was no, thanks, British industry was "quite adequate." Months later, Gross learned that the British were sending a mission to the United States to buy planes after all; the commission would be in California within five days.

In that time, Lockheed's engineers turned out a complete wooden mockup of a reconnaissance bomber adapted from the Lockheed 14. When the British arrived at Burbank, those who liked golf were put up at the Riviera Country Club; those who liked city life were quartered in a midtown hotel. Result of these tactics: Lockheed got a $25 million order for 175 military versions of the Lockheed 14, which the British called Hudsons. It was the largest single order any planemaker had ever received. By spring, Lockheed landed another $65 million order for Hudsons. Said Gross: "That really put us in business."

When war came, Lockheed, like other plane companies, did not merely expand, it exploded. Lockheed's payroll, which had risen to 2,500 workers in 1939, skyrocketed to a peak of 90,000. Its plane-making spread the plants over 7,668,000 square feet of floor space (*versus* 59,600 square feet in 1932). Still there was not enough to take care of the flood of war orders. The assembly line for the Lightning (P-38), a flashy two-engined fighter designed for the Royal Air Force, finally ran out of the shops in a weird S curve. Eventually 30 per cent of Lockheed's production was done outside.

In addition to making its own planes, Lockheed took on a contract for B-17's, and totted up a breath-taking figure for the war years. In all, it turned out $2 billion worth of planes: 2,600 Venturas, a patrol bomber for the Navy; 2,700 Flying Fortresses; 2,900 Hudsons (1,298 for the British); and 9,000 Lightnings (four of the first ten aces in the United States armed forces flew Lightnings) for the United States Army, which took over the British contract. The 19,278 planes Lockheed produced were 6 per cent of United States plane production during the war.

Bob Gross quarterbacked the job . . . but he had and has a crack team to help him. . . . Sometimes one of the players on the team has to pick up one of Bob Gross's fumbles. For example, when the prototype of one of their planes was ready to fly, the engineers estimated that it would take at least seven months to make enough blueprints to get the plane into production. Bob argued: "If you can build one plane from these drawings, why can't you build fifty from them? Let's do it." A few weeks later, plane production was so snarled up from lack of blueprints that a hurry-up call was sent for [brother] Court. When he heard what had happened, he just sighed—and straightened out the tangle.

Yet it was Bob Gross who got Lockheed to perform something like production miracles because he could airily wave away engineers who said that miracles couldn't be done. Back in 1942, he cannily realized that the jet plane was just over the horizon. The Army turned down his offer to build one, figuring that it would be developed too late for World War II. Gross ordered development work, anyhow.

Later, the Army changed its mind and asked for the proto-type of a new jet fighter, to be built in 180 days. Lockheed turned out the prototype of the 550-mile-per-hour Shooting Star in 143 days. When V-J Day came, this was a nice reconversion cushion. The Army kept it in production; it was the only jet fighter being made.

In the same way, Bob Gross took on the job of building the Constellation. Howard Hughes and TWA President Jack Frye wanted a transport plane which would fly farther, faster and carry a bigger load than anything in the air. When Consolidated Aircraft turned down the job, Lockheed accepted it. Then the Army ordered Lockheed to build it for the Air Forces; TWA would have to wait. Thus, when the Army canceled its contracts after V-J day, Lockheed had the plane ready for the airlines.

THE MEN WHO KEEP THEM FLYING [5]

Were he to explore the organizational structure of the airlines [the passenger] . . . would discover that the people concerned with flight operations comprise two major groups: (1) the flight crew and (2) the flight control personnel. And he would discover that the flight crew also includes the flight attendants as well as the men who are at the controls. The flight control personnel include dispatchers and meteorologists. They provide vital information to the flight crew.

The Flight Crew

Once the door is slammed shut and the ramp pulled away, an airliner becomes the responsibility of the flight crew. Up front is the cockpit where the controls are located. This part of the plane today is usually called the "flight deck." Sometimes,

[5] From *Career Opportunities with the Airlines*, pamphlet. Air Transport Association of America. 1000 Connecticut Avenue. Washington 6, D.C. 1957. p 18-49. Reprinted by permission.

too, it is referred to as the "front office," because the captain (the number one pilot, often called simply pilot) is the person in command of the airliner. This is where the captain works—with the copilot and often a flight engineer—amidst a galaxy of knobs, dials, switches and other instruments. The flight deck is separated by a partition, with door, from the main cabin of the airliner. Only authorized airline personnel are allowed to enter this "sanctum sanctorum."

Behind the flight deck is the main cabin. This is the domain of the flight attendants [see "The Woman's Touch," below]. Here are seats for the passengers. In the larger planes there is a galley for serving meals and refreshments aloft. Sometimes, too (especially in international flights) the planes have sleeping compartments. Flight attendants keep the passengers comfortable and serve their needs. They also keep the cabin in order.

The minimum flight crew . . . is made up of pilot, copilot and one flight attendant. In the larger planes . . . the flight crew includes an additional flight attendant and a flight engineer.

The pilot (captain), copilot and flight engineer are directly concerned with the operations of the airliner. They operate the controls and the necessary auxiliary equipment required to get the airliner airborne, keep it on course and return it safely to earth. Only men are employed as airline transport pilots and flight engineers. . . .

Pilots (captains and copilots) and flight engineers are all licensed personnel. They must hold appropriate certificates issued by the Civil Aeronautics Administration (CAA). In order to obtain these permits, pilots, for example, must show evidence of having completed from four hundred to one thousand hours of flying time. One company sets a standard of six hundred hours solo flying time for its flight engineers as well. Another requires that flight engineers have a minimum of four years diversified aircraft and powerplant (aircraft engine) mechanic experience. . . .

The captain of the modern airliner is responsible for the aircraft he flies and for the safety of its passengers and cargo. Like the captain of a ship he is in sole command. His duties are far more than just manipulating the controls, although this is his principal task.

At the controls he is responsible for negotiating takeoffs and landings and maintaining the airliner's true course in terms of the smoothest, safest flying conditions possible. During relief periods when the copilot "takes over control" the captain is also responsible for supervising the actions of the copilot. The captain's decision at all times is law.

Beyond this the captain is responsible for most of the paper work and clearances necessary before an aircraft ever leaves the ground. He must also plot its course and decide upon the best flight plan, the best altitude, the best cruising speed—factors he works out with the flight control personnel prior to takeoff.

The copilot assists or relieves the captain in the operation of the flight controls of an aircraft while under way, including takeoff and landing of such aircraft. His specific responsibilities include checking the progress of the aircraft along its flight route; maintaining vigil over all instruments, and studying weather reports and forecasts. He reports his observations to the captain and keeps an account of the flight in a trip-record book.

The flight engineer operates and supervises the mechanical and electrical devices aboard large aircraft in flight. He controls engine performance in flight, discovers the source of mechanical irregularities in flight, makes emergency repairs, and supervises any mechanical repairs made on aircraft provided at intermediary stations en route.

Since flight-deck personnel are directly responsible for the airliner's mechanical proficiency, their work is highly specialized. Of necessity they are a well integrated group and must operate as a team at peak efficiency. As a general rule, operating flight crews are not permitted to fly more than eighty-five hours in a month on scheduled domestic routes. In addition, provisions are made to assure adequate rest periods for flight crews. On the international systems, it is endeavored to arrange schedules so that flight crews do not fly more than 255 hours in a calendar quarter.

In addition to their flying duties, all flight crew personnel are required to attend classes and take refresher courses to maintain their proficiency ratings and keep abreast of new equipment and changing operational techniques. In addition, they are often called upon to do promotional work for the airline employing them, such as lecturing and other public relations activities. . . .

The Flight Control Personnel

Flight control personnel . . . is comprised of individuals on the ground who are directly concerned with the airliner's flight movements. At all times they work closely with the flight crew in planning and programming the airliner's flight and maintaining close contact with the plane during its entire trip. In a sense they monitor every flight from start to finish. . . .

Only the flight dispatcher within this group is required to have a certificate issued by the Civil Aeronautics Administration. . . . The flight dispatcher authorizes all takeoffs of aircraft and monitors by radio their progress to destination. He is responsible for informing captains en route of developments, such as changing weather, which might affect their flights. He keeps records of the number of aircraft and engines available, keeps a flight log of each under his jurisdiction, and records the load carried by the flights he dispatches. It is also a function of his office to notify crew members of their flight trip assignments. The flight dispatcher must also be able to analyze current weather information obtained from the weather maps and reports of the Weather Bureau. He uses this analysis and the forecast of company and Weather Bureau meteorologists as the basis for all operational plans. He has final authority to approve flight plans. If conditions are such that a flight cannot operate on schedule, he has the responsibility for canceling the flight or authorizing an alternate plan of operation. He must advise all concerned of plans formulated or modified, and he relays plans to other dispatch centers at six-hour intervals.

The duties of the meteorologist require that he be skilled in the use of meteorological instruments and in the preparation of weather maps, charts and diagrams. He must prepare reports on current weather and future forecasts for airline flight personnel and for airline operations and traffic departments. These reports are also made available to Federal Government meteorologists for their use in keeping tab on the weather for the nation as a whole. One of the most important functions of the airline meteorologist is the assistance he gives the dispatcher and pilot in planning a flight. As one pilot puts it, "our 'weather expert' helps us avoid the weather, thereby enabling us to give a smooth flight to our passengers." . . . .

Airline Communications

The modern airliner is an integral part of a varied communications system that includes everything from the telephone and telegraph to railways and roads. All are representative media which people use to communicate with each other. The airliner, however, is dependent upon its own communications system and the people who operate it. . . . The pilot and copilot of the airliner are in radio contact with ground controllers and with other planes in the sky. Voices in the sky feed weather data and other important information to pilots, continuously monitoring the airliner's flight. At the same time, on the ground, a vast interstation teletype network speeds up reservations, weather reports and the transmission of other information necessary to the operations of an airline. All are part of airline communications.

The communications personnel of the scheduled airlines are comprised of ground radio operators and teletype operators. . . . Ground radio employees operate radio facilities at airline stations. When the amount of traffic at a given station is heavy enough, there are additional ground radio operators assigned by the airline, in which event there is a chief ground operator. His responsibilities include transmitting and receiving messages to and from aircraft in flight. He (or one of his staff) relays messages between his company's aircraft and other stations on the route system, communicating with both company dispatch centers and CAA (Civil Aeronautics Administration) air traffic control towers. In addition, the ground radio operator may supervise the operation of automatic recording machines and transcribe, when necessary, the radio messages they record. He must also keep a chronological record of his activities and submit, as required, reports to the station manager.

The teletypist operates the teletype system of the company and receives, transmits and relays messages in accordance with accepted procedures. He handles, delivers and files these messages as required and performs other related duties. . . .

Airline Maintenance

Maintenance people—those who maintain and service aircraft —are the watchdogs over the aircraft making up the scheduled airline fleet and are responsible for their performance and efficiency at all times. Maintenance jobs may be divided into two groups: (1) The aircraft maintenance group comprises those who work directly with the aircraft itself, including the airframe (body and wings), landing gear, controls, electronic equipment, engines, propellers and all the auxiliary equipment necessary to keep the machine in flying condition. (2) The general maintenance group is made up of general shop workers and machine operators who keep the flow of parts, repairs and service operations moving.

The first group breaks down into twelve job categories. In four of these, which are highly specialized, appropriate government certificates or licenses are required. The maintenance employees requiring certificates are airline maintenance inspectors, airframe and powerplant mechanics, aircraft radio technicians and instrument technicians.

The Aircraft Maintenance Inspector. It is the responsibility of the inspector to check and double check the work done by the mechanics and other specialists. Generally he has worked his way up through these various categories. As his title implies, it is his job to inspect the aircraft and all its auxiliary equipment. His final approval is necessary before the aircraft is released for operation. For the most part his work is indoors.

Airframe and Powerplant (Engine) Mechanics. The inspector may be compared to the doctor in that he checks for and analyzes the "disease" or finds the symptoms. The mechanic is the "nurse" who takes care of the patient. In the hangar or out on the line you might find him anywhere—head buried in the engine nacelle [the metal sheathing that covers the engine], fixing the hydraulic system that raises and lowers the landing gear, or deep inside the tail cone of the airliner's body repairing the control cables. He works with skin and frame, with engines, propellers, brakes and wheels. Sometimes he may be called upon to do general maintenance functions—like straightening out a piece of cowling—servicing or inspecting an aircraft. In many cases he also operates the aircraft on the ground—revs up its engines, taxis it from one place to another. He works inside the hangars and shops, or he may be called upon to work outdoors on the ramp in all kinds of weather.

Instrument Technicians. Today's aircraft has a great many instruments—from compass to computer; from fuel gage to pitot tube for measuring the airspeed. Each requires periodic and intricate and delicate care. This is the instrument technician's responsibility—to install, test, repair and overhaul all aircraft, engine and navigational instruments. Sometimes he works inside the aircraft. More often his job finds him in the laboratory amid test instruments and specialized tools.

Radio Technicians. The modern airliner depends upon voices in the sky and on the ground for its communications system, the very heart of an airline's navigational and traffic control system. And radio is the heart of the airliner's communications system. Its function depends not only on the flight people who use it, but on the radio technicians who keep it in perfect condition. They install, maintain, repair and test all aircraft radio equipment. Much of this work is done inside the aircraft. But a lot of laboratory work is also required. . . .

The non-certificated maintenance jobs [mainly] relate directly to aircraft. The propeller specialist must repair and maintain propellers, propeller governors, and related equipment. The electrical and radio assembler joins together the parts and wires of electrical instrument panels. The aircraft welder must be able to use arc or acetylene equipment and work with all kinds of metals. The aircraft painter paints aircraft parts and both the exterior and interior of the aircraft whenever it is necessary. The fabric specialist (upholsterers) covers ailerons and rudders. He also installs fabric linings in aircraft. Aircraft cleaners clean both the interior and exterior of aircraft. The ramp serviceman loads and unloads cargo. When loading, he must distribute cargo according to an appropriate loading chart. He also services the aircraft with fuel and oil or directs such servicing, and maintains the supplies and stock needed for in-flight service. He may be responsible for all ramp service duties. The stockroom clerk or storekeeper receives, stores and issues aircraft parts and supplies. He must keep accurate inventories of such equipment.

The duties of the other non-certificated maintenance employees . . . [machinists, heat treaters, sheet metal workers, shop mechanics, welders, carpenters, electricians, painters, grinder operators, electroplaters, drill press operators, polishers and helpers] —classified as general maintenance personnel—are similar to those performed in other industries.

THE WOMAN'S TOUCH [6]

Birth and death are not ordinary in stewardess experience, but practically every intervening mortal situation is. The stewardess must be a sort of human amalgam. She must be nurse and confidante, maid and mother, teacher, glamour girl and entertainer. She must be decorative and efficient, skilled in conversation, sympathetic in listening. She must care for the sick, reassure the frightened and comfort the unhappy. . . .

Passenger morale is usually in the hands of the stewardess. She can make a flight pleasant or otherwise, allay the passengers' fears in case of bad weather or something worse, or bring on panic. So she must be calm. And certainly she must be courageous. She knows that flying is safe today and she must make the passenger feel that it is too. . . Every stewardess learns early to expect almost anything from her passengers. There are the demanding and the unreasonable. There are the naïve. Just how naïve is sometimes hard to believe. Only recently have the lines stopped passing out chewing gum on takeoffs and landings, to help relieve pressure on the ears.

Many years ago the hostess used to pass out cotton to be packed in the ears against pressure. Mary O'Connor, who has

[6] From "Adventures of the Air-line Stewardesses," article by Henry LaCossitt, journalist and magazine writer. *Saturday Evening Post.* 226:24-5+. June 26, 1954. Reprinted by permission.

been with United as a hostess since 1933, and who even has an airplane named for her, swears that she once carried a group of Indians who ate the cotton and stuck the gum in their ears. . . . Some people are naïve, some are merely odd. A man on a night flight to Dallas hangs up his clothes in the men's room, dons pajamas and, although there are no berths, stretches out for sleep in his seat. A motherly-seeming lady on a trip to New Orleans removes her dress, hangs it up beside her seat, and makes the flight in her slip. . . .

Then there are the amorous people who like to make love at high altitudes, and there are the wolves who think hostesses are their special prey. And there are the gentlemen—with honorable intentions—who find stewardesses irresistible. May Bobeck, former American Airlines hostess, now principal nurse in the company's flight surgeon's office in Chicago, says that she had at least thirty sincere offers of marriage during her seven years as an active stewardess. While most girls today can't match this—partly because few stay in service that long—proposals are common. Marriage is the principal reason for shorter stewardess careers these days. The length of service varies among the lines, but it averages out around two years. Most of the girls marry as a direct result of their jobs. It is estimated that about 30 per cent of them marry company employees, and 21 per cent marry people they have met in flight. And for every marriage there are dozens of near misses and romantic encounters. . . .

For the overseas stewardess, her job is complicated by unfamiliar customs of all sorts. She becomes accustomed to the exotic and learns early that dietary matters, especially, are very important. One TWA girl had to duck a plate of ham and eggs an outraged Moslem threw at her. She had forgotten the pork taboo. It is also very important to know which Hindu is the meat eater and which is the vegetarian, and that many Chinese won't eat an ordinary American menu, but simply love one made up entirely of mangoes, bananas and soft-boiled eggs. Every line carries kosher food for orthodox Jews, whose religion, moreover, will not permit them to travel on their Sabbath—another custom the stewardess must understand. Language is of the first importance on the overseas lines, and both Pan American and TWA—

on overseas runs—require that service personnel have command of at least one foreign language. . . .

All airline officials agree that the stewardess represents service. Because service is one of the chief areas of competition among the lines, the companies increasingly are stressing the importance of the girls. The larger lines, such as American, United, TWA and Pan American, have elaborate systems of recruiting, with teams of personnel experts who cover the United States and Canada in search of hostesses.

The larger lines have their own schools to train the girls in an intensive course of about fifty subjects. At the schools the girls live in dormitories and are subject to discipline like any college girl. The smaller lines draw most of their girls from about fifteen privately operated schools that give courses for prospective airline hostesses. . . .

Physical requirements vary—but not much. They are practically the same whether the girl is trying for American, with its twelve-hundred-stewardess complement—biggest of all the lines —or for Caribbean-Atlantic, which has only seven stewardesses. A stewardess may weigh no more than 135. Her height may be no more than five feet seven inches, no less than five feet one inch. She may be no more than twenty-six years old and no less than twenty-one. She must have perfect vision—no glasses—and health.

These requirements produce a typical stewardess who is twenty-four, weighs 113, and is five feet four and one half inches tall. Because appearance is an important factor, she must have straight teeth and a fortunate complexion. Her figure is "proportioned," another airline requirement. Her hair is short or, if not short, done so that it never falls below the collar of her jacket. There are no requirements as to its color, although some years ago one line—National—decreed that all of its girls should be blondes. This caused talk, produced some odd colors in blondes, and the line was accused of discrimination in restraint of brunettes and redheads. The decree was later rescinded. Another line—Central, which runs from Fort Worth, Texas, to points in Oklahoma — recently issued a ukase declaring that henceforth all of its stewardesses would be full-blooded Indian girls. Nobody complained. All United States lines require that their stewardesses be American citizens or have their first papers, although there are a few exceptions. TWA employs French stewards and stewardesses out of Paris, and Pan American uses some South American girls in flights over that continent. . . .

The typical stewardess has had about two years of college or an equivalent—that is, business or nurses' training, which the lines accept as substitutes. To set off her proportioned figure, she wears a very smart uniform, ordinarily consisting of a skirt and jacket and a pert overseas cap on which is the insigne of her line.

There have been, in all, about forty thousand girls on the lines since 1930, when Ellen Church, a nurse from Cresco, Iowa, first suggested the idea of having a capable woman aboard planes to provide service for passengers. Ellen, now director of nurses at Sherman Hospital in Elgin, Illinois, was hired by United to work their flight between two Western cities, and to recruit other girls for similar duty. She did so and a profession was started.

It is a profession of which its members are extremely proud and in which they have served with distinction. Some have lost their lives in line of duty. Since 1938, when the Civil Aeronautics Board began keeping aviation statistics, sixty-four hostesses have been killed in accidents involving scheduled planes. The figure would be higher, of course, if nonscheduled lines were included.

One of these girls, Mary Frances Housley, of Jacksonville, Florida, has been honored posthumously with a memorial fund in her name. Frankie, as everybody called her, was with National. She was working a flight from New York to Miami in January, 1951, when the plane crashed at Philadelphia's International Airport and caught fire. She led most of the twenty-five passengers to safety. Frankie made eleven trips back into the cabin to help people out. She returned from ten. From the eleventh she did not. The plane was a mass of flames when she went back the last time, but there were two babies and four women still inside. When they found Frankie's body they saw that she had died with one of the babies in her arms. National is using Frankie's fund to help build new nurses' quarters at Miami's Variety Hospital. Frankie was a typical stewardess.

TRAFFIC JAM [7]

Air traffic control, long a worry, has become the bottleneck of aviation. What holds flying back now is not weather, not "speed of sound," not economics, not accidents, but the traffic problem. Airline pilots report, on the average, four "near misses" a day. . . . And so there are committees and round-table discussions and news items. . . .

We've got a form of air traffic control now, of course. It's a nationwide service, part of the machinery of the federally operated system of Civil Airways—the public highways of the air —used by the airlines, by the military, and by business and private planes. But, except near airports, Air Traffic Control governs only blind-flying traffic—airplanes that are inside of clouds. When flying blind the pilot uses an assigned route and altitude and keeps reporting his position. ATC does the rest.

What does it do? First it surrounds each blind-flying airplane with a protective box of air space ten miles broad, one thousand feet high and from twenty-five to one hundred miles long. (Length depends on the airplane's speed. It's ten minutes of flying time.) This box moves along with the airplane. No other aircraft is allowed to enter it, nor is any airplane allowed to enter a cloud or an area of low visibility along Civil Airways without prior approval from ATC.

The pilot nowadays blesses the moment when he is swallowed up by clouds; he can dismiss traffic worries. No United States airliner flying blind with pay passengers has ever had a collision with another aircraft under ATC control. And, despite the increase in traffic, the risk of collision in blind flight is not increasing.

It is the chance of collision in *visual* flight that presents the most serious traffic problem. For the pilot flying "visually"— outside of clouds—there is no air traffic control, except near airports. He is on his own. He must avoid collisions by the old-fashioned method of looking where he's going. To prevent being run down from behind, or rammed from underneath, or sat

[7] From "Big Traffic Jam in the Sky," article by Wolfgang Langewiesche, author of *I'll Take the High Road* and former test pilot for Chance Vought and Cessna Aircraft companies. *Reader's Digest.* 69:49-53. July 1956. Copyright 1956 by The Reader's Digest Association, Inc. Condensed from *Air Facts* June 1956. Reprinted by permission.

down upon from above, he has to trust the other fellow to look where *he* is going! This goes for any airplane, even the mighty airliner.

That brings in the possibility of slackness. Many pilots still have a lingering notion that the air is normally empty. This is understandable; most of the time it *looks* as empty as it used to be. But now suddenly, too often, somebody is right there—full size. Also, the modern airplane is flown mostly by instruments and paper work; the pilot can't be looking outside more than about half the time.

As airplanes grow faster, and as there are more of them, the chance grows that somebody will come too close "between looks." Even if the pilots see each other they may not be able to avoid colliding.

There is still another problem. Planes flying blind get good protection, up to a point. The point is this: ATC can no longer handle all the blind-flying traffic that *wants* to be handled. Because each blind-flying plane must be surrounded by that big box of space, the air's traffic-carrying capacity drops to a fraction when it turns cloudy. It is as if there were a law that, while it rains, a driver must keep half a mile behind the car ahead. At metropolitan airports incoming flights often have to wait and circle, or have to be diverted to other cities. Others are held on the ground until there is air space for them. All this is expensive for the airlines and annoys the passenger.

The situation will get worse, for the airlines have all those jets on order. Jets can't tolerate traffic delays; they would run out of fuel. And they can't fit into present traffic control procedures —an aerial standing-in-line, with step-by-step descent toward the airport. They have to stay at twenty thousand feet till Control can guarantee them a landing; then come down in one fast swoop, through all other traffic. This seems an impossible control task with present methods.

The root of the trouble lies in that private box of air space around each blind-flying airplane. Away from the vicinity of the airports it's much too big—perhaps one hundred times as much as is needed in visual flight. But with present methods the box *has* to be big, for safety. For the airplane does not always stay nicely in the middle of its box: it may get right to the wall of it, almost over in somebody else's box!

Here is how it goes. The pilot figures out where he is, and when he will be where next. He reports by radiotelephone to a station somewhere under him where the operator relays the message to the nearest air route traffic control center. Controllers there keep track of hundreds of planes. If there is conflict, they issue new instructions by phone to the ground station, whose operator then calls the pilots and gives each his message: A is to "hold" north and west of point X while B climbs through A's altitude to get out of C's way; B is to report leaving A's altitude; A is to expect further clearance at 1407 o'clock.

All this proceeds at a terrific pace; messages are clipped, abbreviated to save seconds. An airline captain recently published a radio log of a typical Washington-Boston nonstop flight. The flight required thirty-three radio contacts—one every three minutes and forty seconds. You can see how many chances there are for errors. Watching a pilot at work, you can see why the box has to be big.

At the ground station the need for space is even more clear. Here the harassed operator is listening to several radios at once, the military, the airlines, the general traffic, each using a different frequency. In the clouds above him there may be fifteen airplanes, flying blind, at different altitudes—and he has business with all of them. Several voices often talk at the same time.

A good "communicator" can speak one message while he listens to another and jots it down. But even if you are a good communicator you have headaches. If the man you want to reach is not tuned in on you, it is difficult to contact him. And while you use that radio frequency it is blocked for other pilots. If two pilots talk at the same time, both are garbled. Small delays can quickly build up into big delays. Pilot X must be told to change altitude to keep from getting too close to pilot Y; but suppose there's a three-minute delay in reaching X? In three minutes he moves perhaps twelve miles. So the box is not big without reason.

When the blind-flying airplane gets into the approach zone of a big airport the box shrinks to three miles by three miles by one thousand feet. This is because the approach controller can watch his traffic on radar and talk with the pilots direct. But there are so many airplanes converging on those airports that the lack of air space is just as bad, and the radio congestion worse.

In the airport control tower itself the situation is superficially different but essentially the same. Now everybody can see, airplanes can fly closer together, control is faster—but so is the action.

And it still depends on brain, language, radio, plus the human eye, which is not infallible. A pilot reports himself "three miles southwest" when he should say "southeast." A controller sees two airplanes of the same make, and has to waste time finding out which one is which: "Cessna one-two-Charlie, please rock your wings." Two pilots talk at the same time and garble each other. A control tower is like a parrot cage, crazy with voices.

That's the way it is with blind-flying control, when the weather puts a limit on the number of planes that want to fly. When you try to extend traffic control into clear air, you deal at one stroke with perhaps twenty times the traffic, and that makes the control job perhaps four hundred times as tough. Look at an air route after the clouds have cleared: you see test flights, ferry flights, training flights, military and civil. You see crop-dusting, pipe-line patrols, aerial mapping, forest-fire patrol; people going places for a thousand and one reasons. And these are only a small percentage of those who would be flying if the traffic jam didn't keep them out of the air.

One of the most disastrous effects of the traffic problem is that it chokes off flying that would otherwise be done. One example: the airlines would like to offer shuttle service between, say, New York and Washington, D.C.: a flight every ten minutes, no reservations, just go to the airport and get on. It can't be done; in bad weather ATC simply wouldn't have the space. The same goes for helicopter commuting service, or short-haul service.

Aside from military aviation, the worst choke is on "general aviation"—that flying which is neither airline nor military, but is simply the use of airplanes by all sorts of people, car-like. Even now this is the biggest part of aviation, as to number of airplanes, number of pilots, hours flown, miles flown. But it is nothing compared to what it should be. After the war the CAA forecast 400,000 civil airplanes in the United States by now. Instead there are 58,000, and a third of these are inactive.

The reason: the traffic problem. It effectively bars 75 per cent of all airplanes from flying in clouds, and has kept the biggest part of American aviation where the airlines were twenty-five years ago. Because of traffic the metropolitan areas are today inaccessible in weather that used to be easily flyable. This is not good enough for a machine that is supposed to save time. So hundreds of thousands of airplanes remain unbuilt. An industry that should be big and growing is only an infant one.

This is doubly galling because the weather itself, apart from traffic angles, is practically licked. Today the airline pilot, technically, can fly and land in weather that grounded him fifteen years ago. The Air Force is just about an all-weather outfit. With modern instruments and radio devices, even the nonprofessional can fly blind with ease, and handle most types of weather. But the traffic control snarl robs us of the victory.

What can be done about it? There is air space enough for a million airplanes, if the control of them can be made lightning-quick and continuous. At each regional ATC office we need to have an electronic computer. Into it, information about each airplane must be fed by quick electric impulses, and from a source that's more reliable than the harassed brain of the pilot. Out of this computer must come instant, continuous orders to each pilot, shown in the cockpit perhaps by red and green signal lights and arrows. With such a system, flight through clouds becomes available to all, and clear air can be traffic-controlled and still remain available to all.

WHEN THE PLANE FALLS [8]

One night in February [1952], scant minutes after the sleeping city of Elizabeth, New Jersey, was jolted by its third plane crash in two months—a crash actuaries insist was mathematically

[8] From "Air-Crash Detective at Work," by Richard Witkin, aviation editor of the New York *Times*. *Collier's*. 130:15-18. August 2, 1952. Copyright 1952 by The Crowell-Collier Publishing Company. Reprinted by permission.

impossible—a short, husky man with a photographer in tow bounded upstairs to the top floor of a burning three-story apartment house.

Hoping to get pictures before fire destroyed the evidence, Joseph O. Fluet, regional chief of the Civil Aeronautics Board's safety investigation bureau, raced down a hallway toward the flames, stopped the first fireman he met and asked if he had any idea where the airliner had hit the building.

Over the uproar the fireman barked: "What damn' difference does it make now? This wouldn't have happened if you guys gave a hoot about the people on the ground." Fluet, who, ironically enough, had been able to get to the scene so quickly only because he was in Elizabeth investigating crash No. 2, replied patiently. "Look, bud," he said, "you don't feel any worse than I do. I'm doing a job same as you." Silently the man helped Fluet find the parapet where the right wing had struck, cartwheeling the plane into an orphanage yard across the way.

Down by the wreckage, Fluet had to buck the human element again. A woman bystander with a blanket over her arm sneered: "Why don't you stupid phonies close down Newark Airport before the rest of our homes get bashed in?" A man holding a small boy shouted: "What are we supposed to do, sit around waiting for the next one to hit the orphanage?" . . .

As the public clamor spread across the nation, a jittery aviation industry overnight rustled together a top-echelon committee, called the National Air Transport Co-ordinating Committee, composed of presidents of major air lines and other key aviation agencies . . . to take immediate steps toward greater air safety over congested areas [and] President Truman named a three-man special committee . . . to survey the entire problem of airport planning. But meanwhile the Elizabeth crashes themselves had to be investigated. The dates of the three disasters were December 16, January 22 and February 11. By mid-March, Fluet—a forty-five-year-old pilot-mechanic with an anatomy professor's knowledge of a plane's innards—had completely solved the first and the third. On the second, though stopped short of a conclusive answer, he had spotlighted an alarming "possible cause." This brought changes in wiring of the propeller system in the plane model involved.

Fluet achieved these swift results despite time out to testify before grand juries, explain the science of crash detection on radio and TV, address luncheon clubs, conduct congressional committees on tours of the crash sites and sandwich in a probe of a fourth major crash in his Northeast region on January 14 (that of a Northeast Airlines Convair which, enroute from Boston, slithered through fog into New York's East River, less than half a mile short of its La Guardia Airport goal).

Fluet's bailiwick covers Virginia to Maine, as well as overseas crashes of planes based in that area. Because his region is the most heavily traveled, he can generally count on the heaviest work-load of all eight CAB regional offices. But actually the number of fatal airline crashes is very small . . . and a regional office seldom has to handle more than two or three major investigations annually. Most of its time is spent checking on nonfatal airline mishaps—and on its share of the national total of four thousand to five thousand accidents a year involving private planes.

The CAB Investigation

Thus the freak spate of four airline disasters in four months which confronted Fluet not only flouted the law of averages but made him indisputably the busiest air sleuth in history. The CAB, created by Congress to make the rules governing American aviation, also operates as a nation-wide safety investigation bureau. Its thirty-eight investigators have developed a standard detection system so efficient—they've cracked 85 per cent of the fatal and over 95 per cent of the nonfatal airline crashes—that it has been adopted by many other countries.

The system is in essence based on no more than the painstaking process of elimination. But before Joe Fluet can set about eliminating possible causes of a crash—engine failure, generator fire, pilot error—he must take prompt precautions to seal off the mass of evidence from which he hopes to reconstruct the pattern of disaster. Fluet's first move, when word of a crash is flashed to him, is to phone nearest police headquarters and order the wreckage roped off and guarded against looters and souvenir hunters. Move number two is to dispatch his aides to the spot to double-check on security, interview witnesses and collar all immediate evidence they can find.

The "process of elimination" which Fluet sets in motion, after the preliminary precautions in all crash cases, begins at whatever local hall he has lined up for his headquarters the morning after a crash has occurred. By then, a corps of specialists will have poured in—from the airline concerned, the CAB, the plane, engine and propeller manufacturers, and also from the Civil Aeronautics Administration (the agency that enforces CAB rules and operates the airport control towers and other facilities of the aerial highways).

Fluet divides the corps, over which he has full jurisdiction, into teams of four or five: one to work on engines, one to look for structural failures, one to seek clues in the electrical system, one to study the plane's records, and one to interview eyewitnesses. In addition, he will launch a dozen special tests prompted by the special nature of the particular crash, such as an autopsy on the pilots, or a metallurgy test on a sheared rudder assembly, or a chemical analysis of burn marks on a plane tire.

The "team" procedure is followed in every major inquiry, even if the cause of the crash seems as obvious as a man standing over a murder victim with a smoking gun in his hand. Most inquiries, Fluet has found, will turn up an accessory to the crime: overloading, pilot error, malfunction of an emergency system. . . .

Fluet was at his home in Great Neck, Long Island, on the Sunday afternoon . . . when word of the first Elizabeth crash was phoned to him from the CAA office at La Guardia. All that the CAA knew was that a C-46 Curtis Commando—believed to be operated by Miami Airlines Inc., a "nonsked" [nonscheduled] outfit—had just plowed in about seven miles southwest of Newark. . . . Fluet hopped in his official car and headed for the scene.

Wreckage Showed None Had Survived

He knew as soon as he saw the wreckage that none of the fifty-six on board could have survived. But fortunately the plane had dropped into virtually the only uncluttered area in the business center— a narrow stretch where the shallow Elizabeth River ambles between two solidly built-up blocks. As a result, no one on the ground had been killed, only one person injured. The local citizenry was less indignant than relieved that it hadn't been worse.

The morning after the crash, Fluet organized his teams and started shuttling between the scene, the courthouse and the detection lab. In the evenings, he threshed over the day's gleanings with team leaders in their rooms in the Winfield Scott Hotel.

Since it was known that the right engine had caught fire, the engine team was the main focus of attention. Piece by piece, the battered right engine was dismantled. It was a slow process, requiring use of acetylene torches, special hammers, bolt cutters, snips, odd-size wrenches and delicately rigged pulling equipment.

Hours were consumed disengaging a badly damaged piston assembly from a distorted and partly molten cylinder. Each part was examined to see if it had been burned in the air or only after the plane struck the ground. Working from the rear of the engine forward, Fluet sought to chart the course of the blaze as the slip stream whipped the flames backward from their point of origin—the point where the "something" he was looking for had gone wrong.

The investigators hammered away for a week, removing the exhaust, fuel and oil pumps, carburetor and numberless other parts. Finally, they came to the end of the line—the No. 10 cylinder. Nothing forward of that cylinder had been burned before the plane crashed. Plainly the fire had got its start at that point. The technical division of the CAB in Washington examined the cylinder and found that the real culprits were the fifteen bolt assemblies that hold a cylinder to its moorings. They had failed, and the cylinder had broken loose, allowing gas to spurt onto the red-hot engine.

Fluet tied up the investigation on January 11 and hastened home . . . . Three days later came the Convair crash into the East River; luckily, the thirty-six people aboard escaped death. According to the information disclosed during the public hearing, Fluet's investigation indicated that the pilots had misjudged the approach to nearby La Guardia because of poor visibility.

Eight days after that crash, Fluet had to move back to Elizabeth. An American Airlines Convair carrying twenty-three persons—including former Secretary of War Robert P. Patterson—fell out of ragged rain clouds into a row of houses only a few blocks from the first crash point. All on board were killed instantly, and this time there was no escape for the ground-borne citizenry. Seven residents of the houses were killed and nine hospitalized. For the first time, public clamor to shut down Newark Airport reached serious proportions. Committees were formed, protest meetings held, and legislators poured into town for a firsthand look.

Fluet rolled up his sleeves and went hunting for clues. The inquiry was destined to be the only one of the Elizabeth trilogy that would refuse to yield a hard-and-fast answer. But he managed to rule out all except two possible causes, one of which led to radical new safety precautions.

All that was known—from radar—was that the Convair had been making a normal approach through the soup when it suddenly swerved to the right and plunged to the ground. Both of Fluet's possibilities assumed that the swerve to the right must have been caused by trouble in the right engine. That would have allowed the good left engine to pull the plane to the right.

One theory was that the pilot may have forgotten to apply carburetor heat, and that ice formed in the carburetor and choked off the gas supply. The other was that a short circuit twisted the right propeller blades momentarily from normal to reverse angle. That would mean that the propeller, instead of grabbing air and pulling the plane forward, started backwatering furiously like a ferry-boat just before it docks. The airline was so alarmed over the prop-reversal theory that it ordered propeller wires isolated from all other wiring and covered with extra insulation to make a short circuit virtually impossible.

Only twenty days after the second Elizabeth crash, the impossible occurred: a third airliner—a National Airlines DC-6 bound from Newark Airport for Miami—plummeted into Elizabeth, hit an apartment house and landed into an orphanage play yard. Twenty-nine of the sixty-three persons aboard were killed.

Four apartment-house tenants died as the plane spewed flaming gas through their windows. Seven others on the ground were injured.

Fluet had been asleep about an hour when word was flashed to his hotel room a few minutes after midnight. He is convinced that if the authorities had not closed down Newark airport voluntarily, Elizabeth residents would have carried out threats to close it themselves by sitting on the runways.

It was in this crisis atmosphere that Fluet set about determining what had crippled the DC-6. For clues, he had an emergency message from the pilot—"I lost an engine, am coming back"—and a flight path showing the plane had veered to the right.

If the pilot had simply lost one of his four engines, he should not have had any trouble coming around for an emergency landing. Fluet knew something else must have gone wrong. The swerve to the right focused attention at the outset on the two right engines. Fluet and his engine team examined the propeller settings. For it was logical to assume that, if either or both the right engines had conked out, the pilot would have tried to feather them—that is, turn the propeller directly into the wind to minimize air-speed-killing drag.

What Study of Propellers Revealed

Though the propellers were twisted like pretzels and had snapped in several places, complicated measuring instruments made it possible to determine at what angle each blade had been set at the moment of impact.

Fluet and his crew discovered first that the right outboard propeller was, in fact, feathered. That accounted for one engine lost—as the pilot had radioed. They next set about measuring the blade settings on the right inboard propeller. Several of the team suspected that they would find this propeller feathered also. But they found something far more interesting. They found all the blades—except one small fragment—in reverse pitch, indicating that the engine had been using its hundreds of horsepower to backwater. No wonder the plane had been unable to keep flying!

One dissenting opinion came from the propeller manufacturer. The company pointed to the one blade fragment that was found in normal—not reverse—pitch. It argued that this fragment, found in the apartment house, must have struck the parapet first, and that the force of the blow twisted the other blades into reverse.

But Fluet gathered evidence in an effort to refute this theory. Some of the tests involved would tax the understanding of a *summa cum laude* in engineering. To cite just one example: mathematicians figured out the speed with which the propellers would have had to change pitch—if the company's theory were right. The first blade to hit the apartment house would have been at 29 degrees positive—or normal—pitch, and the blow would have been powerful enough to twist the second blade to 18 degrees negative—or reverse—pitch by the time this second blade struck the parapet.

That would have meant a 47-degree blade twist in the time it took the roaring propeller to turn one third of a revolution. Assuming that the propeller was turning at a normal 2,600 revolutions per minute, it could have meant a 47-degree twist in 17/1,000 of a second—90 times the normal maximum rate. It would also have meant that hydraulic oil in the blade-twisting system would have had to spurt through an opening no larger than the head of a pencil at the rate of 692 gallons a minute. Fluet and his teams concluded that such speeds were, to say the least, highly unlikely.

Two days after the crash, the CAA ordered the same corrective measures on all DC-6's that American Airlines already had taken on their Convairs after crash No. 2. Prop-reversal wires were ordered isolated from all other wiring to prevent short circuits. . . .

Looking back on the Elizabeth debacle, Fluet draws consolation from the fact that it forced the industry to stop and look at the weaknesses it had noticed only in passing in the wild scramble for progress. The outraged public was considerably mollified by the prompt measures taken to steer traffic away from congested areas. The improving climate was manifest when a cargo plane smashed into a crowded section of Jamaica, Long

Island, on April 5 [1952] after missing an over-the-water approach to Idlewild. (Fluet managed to trace the crash to a defective part deep in the bowels of the left engine.) There was a resurgence of close-the-airport agitation, but it never really caught on.

Sometimes, sitting at his desk at the edge of New York's Idlewild airport watching the silver airliners stream in and out, Fluet wishes that science would give the poor human being a break. He wishes it would let the commercial pilot get comfortable in the cockpit of his new three-hundred-mile-an-hour plane before routing him out and tossing him into a four-hundred-mile-an-hour jet.

"But with the world situation as it is," he admits, "we've got to keep up with the parade. . . . In a couple of years, jets will be streaming in here at four-hundred miles an hour, knocking traffic control into a cocked hat. New safety problems on our necks just when we're starting to feel we've got the situation in hand. There's only one way we'll lick them. Start planning now."

THE CURTIS REPORT [9]

The airplane has become the prime mover of our population in its circulation over distances beyond two hundred miles. There has been no serious lack of foresight in our seizing upon the opportunities presented by the air. We have developed 158,000 miles of airways over continental United States, and our aircraft population [number of planes using the airways] has grown from 29,000 in 1936 to 90,000 today. By 1975 we expect the United States aircraft population to increase to 125,000.

As these aircraft become more versatile, productive, and dependable, they are flown more each year. While in 1936 there were 5 million takeoffs and landings at the nation's airports, there are now 65 million, and 115 million are forecast for 1975. . . .

[9] From "Traffic Control in Crowded Skies," by Edward Peck Curtis, vice president of Eastman Kodak Company and lately special assistant to President Eisenhower for aviation facilities planning. *Atlantic Monthly.* 200:118-19. October 1957. Reprinted by permission. (This article is a résumé of his report to the President as head of a special committee to formulate a national plan for safety in the air.)

Actually there is no shortage of airspace for any demand that can now be foreseen. Our problem is an obsolescent traffic control system which was never designed to cope with the complex mixture of civil and military traffic that now fills the air. So intense is the pressure, especially around the major metropolitan centers, that a drastic rationing of airspace will soon be inescapable unless we install a more efficient system of traffic control. . . .

By 1975 the airport capacity of the country must be doubled, and the number of aircraft under traffic control will increase by ten times.

Allocation of Airlanes

1. We are convinced that aircraft depending solely on pilot vision and alertness to avoid collision cannot safely share the same segments of airspace as those aircraft which are kept separate by air traffic control. The plan envisions, therefore, division of the airspace into zones.

2. First, all airspace above a designated altitude will be set aside for controlled separation at all times, because visibility and speeds at higher altitudes are such as to make "see-and-be-seen" flight unsafe.

3. Below this upper zone, a further division of airspace will be made. Funnels and cylinders of airspace are reserved for controlled separation of aircraft traveling from the upper zone to airports. Separate traffic patterns, final approach lanes, and separate runways will, whenever practical, be provided for high and low performance aircraft either at the same airport or adjacent to it. Highways of controlled airspace connecting the funnels and cylinders are reserved for controlled separation of low-flying traffic.

4. Airspace outside the highways, funnels, and cylinders is reserved for aircraft capable of visual collision avoidance.

5. For flight in see-and-be-seen airspace, aircraft must meet accepted minimum cockpit visibility requirement. They must be flown below a designated airspeed and carry a barometric altimeter to determine altitude boundaries of controlled airspace. It may also be necessary for see-and-be-seen aircraft to carry a simple electronic device to detect the edges of controlled airspace.

6. The paths required by the users vary with type of aircraft, length of flight, and weather and wind conditions. For short-distance flights between population centers, fixed paths will be used.

7. Transcontinental flights, on the other hand, will have flexible paths to take advantage of the most favorable flying conditions. These flights commonly take place at high altitudes where they do not interfere with traffic on the fixed paths.

8. Direct flights between minor population centers are a small percentage of the total traffic and tend to spread out over the whole country. Thus, in any particular area, the density of this type of traffic will be very low, and separation can be provided without undue complication.

9. For flights inbound into terminal areas, descending paths that converge on the airport are required. Also, inbound aircraft must maneuver so that they will be lined up and ready for the final approach at the correct altitude and airspeed. The path an aircraft follows during this maneuvering process will combine descent with horizontal path stretching in such a way that aircraft reach their destination in a sequence with other aircraft landing at the same terminal. Ascending paths will be provided for outbound flights.

Traffic Control

Control of air traffic will be carried out by a central ground authority by continuous prearrangement of airspace reservation for each aircraft, as contrasted to free flow of traffic with the control system intervening occasionally to resolve potential conflicts. The airspace will be divided up further into blocks of airspace defined electronically by a navigation system, and used as a basis of defining airspace reservation.

The air situation will be determined by the air traffic control system by two independent methods: reporting of position by the aircraft, and a three-dimensional ground surveillance system. The position data from these two sources will be correlated by air traffic controllers to determine flight progress and to assign clear airspace in the process of air traffic control.

Communication will be essentially automatic between all elements of the system, thus eliminating the delays encountered today because of the delays in voice communication. Voice communication, however, will remain the basic emergency means of communication throughout the system in case of equipment failure, and for those operators who do not, because of the expense involved, install cooperating automatic communication equipment.

Control will be decentralized, with each controller having a display of the airspace under his jurisdiction tailored to fit the geometry of his airspace. Data will be concentrated and organized to suit the functions of each controller. The human controller should—and can—retain his vital role as the decision-making element of the system.

But the processing, storage, communication, and display of data used to make the decisions will be thoroughly mechanized. Additionally, automatic devices will be used to carry out calculations to facilitate scheduling and to expedite the flow of traffic.

SAFETY IN THE AIR [10]

Eight years ago the Radio Technical Commission for Aeronautics, a quasi-governmental organization, prepared the blueprint for what it called an "ultimate" air-traffic control system, a dazzling wonder, full of radar, computers, and flashing lights. The commission's recommendations eventually became the official policy of the United States Government, and the special committee that did the work was presented with the 1948 Collier Trophy. But nothing ever came of the idea. Nothing ever came of a stream of similar ideas.

Now, at last, it would appear that something is going to be done. The tragic crash in the Grand Canyon was a vivid portent of what will happen if something isn't done, and the public has become aware that time has run out. [On June 30, 1956, a United Air Lines DC-7B and a TWA Constellation, both flying east "by eyesight," collided over the Grand Canyon. Toll: 143 dead, no survivors.—Ed.] Before commercial jets start flying the

[10] From "The Price of Air Safety," by Edmund L. Van Deusen, associate editor of *Fortune*. *Fortune*. 54:144-8+. Reprinted by special permission from the September 1956 issue of *Fortune* magazine. Copyright 1956 by Time Inc.

airways in late 1958, the United States must have a traffic system that maintains "positive control" of all aircraft at all times, good weather and bad.

But there is a hard fight ahead. Getting an effective air-traffic control system is not simply a matter of more money and energy; whatever action the government may shortly take, there will still be tough technical questions to be resolved and serious conflicts of interest as well. Positive control would, for one thing, obsolete most of the present air control system. This would be no great loss, but as to what system should replace it there is very little agreement. Then there is the effect of positive control on the swarms of private fliers. The military and the airlines would benefit under positive control; most private fliers, however, for reasons of cost or lack of experience, simply cannot fly by any control system at all. Indeed, fewer than 7 per cent of the 300,000 trained pilots in the United States, commercial and private, are able to fly today's bad-weather control system. Positive control may be ahead, but it is going to remain just there, ahead, until these conflicts are resolved.

Right now the United States has no traffic control except around airports and when the weather turns bad. Under normal conditions every plane in the sky is allowed to fly pretty much as it pleases, controlled only by the Visual Flight Rules. These, in effect, mean that in clear weather, when the pilot can "see and be seen," it's up to the pilot to avoid other planes—which is very much like being controlled by no rules at all. Only when visibility falls below three miles, which is less than 15 per cent of the time, do the more stringent Instrument Flight Rules go into effect. It is only then that pilots must start reporting their positions to one of the twenty-six Air Route Traffic Control Centers of the Civil Aeronautics Administration, where controllers use the reports to maintain minimum distances between craft that are flying in their districts. Under Instrument Flight control, collisions—or even "near-collisions"—between aircraft are virtually unknown.

Bad weather is not the problem. In the past decade there have been over two hundred mid-air collisions involving civil aircraft over the United States, about half of them fatal (84 per cent of the collisions have been between private planes). Nearly all of the collisions have occurred, like the Grand Canyon crash, in *clear weather,* when theoretically, at least, each plane could "see and be seen." Similarly, bad weather is rarely a factor in near-collisions, now averaging four a day according to a recent airline study. (The definition of a "near-collision" is another controversy. Private fliers claim that airline pilots often stretch the definition to include routine passes. The pilots maintain they report only dangerous near misses.)

The "see and be seen" concept on which Visual Flight Rules are based is clearly outdated. As the Grand Canyon crash proved, even propeller-driven planes are now flying too fast to see and be seen with safety. Jets will make the problem far more acute. Two jet planes flying on a collision course at five hundred miles per hour need to see each other two miles apart if they are to pass safely. If they are only one mile apart, and closing at a thousand feet or more a second, there is nothing the pilots can do to avoid disaster.

Congressional committees investigating the Grand Canyon crash have found no shortage of schemes and devices that could be used in a round-the-clock, all-weather traffic control system. Some of these are based on extensive use of radar; others, on television; still others, on automatic telemetering of air information to central ground control stations. Giant computers have been designed to ring bells and light lights in the ground control stations every time two aircraft head toward each other.

Any all-weather, positive control system is almost certain to cost upwards of $2 billion, and a basic-patent position on any part of this huge system would be worth millions. . . .

The government has been doing a great deal of research itself. For seventeen years the Civil Aeronautics Administration has maintained a Technical Development Center at Indianapolis, and most of the techniques and instruments used today in the Instrument Flight control system were originally developed there. Independent of this work, the Air Force has been spending at least $5 million a year on the development of its own TRACALS system (Traffic Control, Approach, and Landing System). Out of this effort have come such astonishing pieces of hardware as the Volscan radar computer. Volscan can fasten onto approaching aircraft forty to sixty miles from the airport and guide them toward the final-approach "gate" so that the planes touch the landing strip at precise thirty-second intervals. This rate, equivalent to 120 landings per hour, is two or three times greater than the best that human controllers can accomplish, even with the help of radar.

Bureaucratic Indecision

Why has so little of this new technology been put to use? Much of the blame has been laid to simple bureaucratic confusion. There is plenty of it: more than seventy-five governmental committees, commissions, departments, and coordinators have a voice in air-control matters. This bureaucratic confusion, however, is primarily a reflection of a failure by both the Congress and the Administration to decide what exactly are the government's responsibilities in matters of traffic safety, and how it should resolve the interests of the conflicting parties.

The present air-traffic control system had its start in the barnstorming 1920's when the Bureau of Lighthouses took on the job of providing searchlights and radio beacons to guide aircraft through the night. This was purely a navigational service, similar to what is provided for rivers and harbors, and no attempt was made to keep aircraft from hitting each other. Eventually, however, traffic on certain routes reached such a density that some sort of control was necessary, and the airlines themselves banded together to provide this service. Starting in 1935, airline-operated control centers were established at Newark, Cleveland, and Chicago.

In 1936, however, the government recognized that it had certain responsibilities in this field and control functions were given to the Department of Commerce. In 1938 the control was delegated to the new Civil Aeronautics Authority, an independent agency. In 1940 the CAA was split in two; to make the rules, there was an independent Civil Aeronautics Board; to carry the rules out, there was a truncated CAA, which was once again part of the Commerce Department.

To keep harmony between the government's interests in civil and in military aviation, an interdepartmental Air Coordinating Committee was created in 1946. In 1948 an Air Navigation Development Board was created to serve as ACC's technical arm. The board's job was to create the equipment for a "common" air-traffic control system that would meet the needs of very segment of the air population.

The cast of characters was now complete for a bureaucratic tragedy. The interests and ambitions of private, commercial, and military aviators were just too different for any coordinating organization to resolve. Caught in between the two groups, the new board never had a chance. The organization is still officially alive, but as General Milton W. Arnold, vice president of the Air Transport Association, told a House committee in July, "We need merely to have the formal funeral. The group's failure has lain in a basic deficiency of its organization. Unless there is agreement between the two voting members—Commerce and Defense—there can be no decision, and thus relatively little progress."

The particular problem on which ANDB finally seems to have foundered involves only one part of a traffic control system, the technique used for providing aircraft with short-range navigation guidance. But this problem well illustrates the deep division between Commerce and Defense as to how the nation's air space is to be controlled.

TACAN versus *VOR-DME*

The navigation trouble started shortly after World War II when the CAA began replacing its old four-course radio ranges with the new VOR (Very-High-Frequency Omni-directional Radio Range) units developed by the Indianapolis Technical Development Center. These were a tremendous improvement over the earlier devices since the high frequency eliminated the static that used to drown out the old signals precisely when they were needed most. Moreover, the pilot could now tell, within three degrees, the direction to the transmitter. He therefore had an infinity of courses he could fly relative to the transmitter instead of the old four courses leading only to adjoining stations. Finally, in 1952, the CAA began installing Distance Measuring Equipment (DME) at the VOR locations; aircraft equipped with both DME and VOR units could tell, by bouncing a radio signal to the DME unit on the ground and measuring the time it took to get back, their exact location in space. The makings were now available for the first precise traffic control system.

Meanwhile another navigation system was being developed that, although different technically, would be almost exactly the same as VOR-DME in function. From the start the Navy had been unhappy with VOR because its ground antenna seemed too big and clumsy to mount on an aircraft carrier. By going to an even higher frequency, a smaller transmitter could be devised. Moreover, by using certain techniques known to scientists but never tried, it was theoretically possible to make a navigation aid three times as accurate as VOR. For carrier pilots searching out a single dot in a big ocean, this extra accuracy would be a big help. Finally, the higher frequency made it possible to combine direction-indicating with distance-measuring in a single unit (although at the cost of a communication channel available on VOR). To get all these advantages in one unit, the Navy underwrote a major research effort by the Federal Telecommunication Laboratories of I. T. & T. [International Telephone and Telegraph Corporation]. By 1951 the new device had been given a name, TACAN (Tactical Air Navigation), and the Air Force had joined the Navy in support of the project.

But TACAN was still wrapped in security and meanwhile CAA was proceeding with VOR and DME. Eventually over 360 ground stations were equipped with transmitters for both devices and many military planes and virtually every airliner were equipped with airborne VOR units. A cheap (under $1,000) VOR unit was developed for private fliers and over 34,000 of them were sold. When DME became available, the same pattern of acceptance seemed ready to repeat itself.

But then, in early 1954, the armed forces suddenly faced up to the fact that they could hardly plan on using VOR-DME during peacetime domestic flights over the continental United States and TACAN in tactical battlefield situations, for these too might be over the continental United States. Planes would have to be equipped with two sets of heavy, expensive navigation gear, and, even more important, the two systems are not compatible in the same air space; DME and TACAN both use the same frequency bands and would jam each other if operated side by side.

By then, however, the military were committed to over $175 million worth of TACAN research and equipment. With almost brusque haste, the military took the wraps off TACAN and insisted that it be made the single system for the domestic United States. In the resulting Donnybrook, all implementation of airborne DME came to a halt.

There is still no final decision on the fight between the two systems, although it now seems inevitable that a compromise will be worked out. VOR and TACAN, without its distance-measuring feature, will be allowed to coexist; meanwhile, DME units will slowly change, over the course of a decade, from the CAA to the TACAN type. The only fact on which there appears to be total agreement is that any such compromise would be far less desirable than a system based on all VOR-DME or all TACAN. [In September 1958 CAA awarded a contract to the International Telephone and Telegraph Corporation for 132 VORTAC ground stations in the United States, and 1,098 more are contemplated. See "The Civil Aeronautics Board and the Civil Aeronautics Administration" in this section, above.—Ed.]

While the TACAN-VOR fight raged, more and faster planes were taking to the air. Moreover, the airlines had gone on a jet-plane buying spree and there was general agreement that before the jets were put into service something had to be done about the Visual Flight situation. Reports came from Europe that pilots of Comet airliners shuttling between London and Rome had never once seen each other even though they often passed close by. In the United States a jet bomber accidentally passed through a formation of what the pilot thought to be three other jets, nicking the tail of one, only to learn later that it had been a formation of six and that no one in the formation, even on the plane hit, had known of the intrusion.

Late last year [1955] Commerce Secretary Weeks decided some action was needed. In December he fired out of hand the head of CAA, Fred Lee, and replaced him with Charles J. Lowen Jr., a Denver businessman. Lowen immediately instituted an ambitious five-year plan that would quadruple the agency's present use of radar and at the same time extend the direct-communication channels between pilots and controllers (at present, in most parts of the country, pilot messages must be relayed through airline or CAA radio operators). In January a special investigating committee for the Bureau of the Budget came up with the predictable conclusion that a central authority was needed if any sense was to be made of the government's many aviation interests. In February, President Eisenhower appointed Edward P. Curtis, former air ace and presently vice president of Eastman Kodak, to the new post of special presidential assistant for aeronautics. Curtis was charged with the job of determining (1) what the nation's air-traffic needs will be ten to twenty years from now, (2) how these needs can best be met, and (3) what sort of government organization will best guarantee that the job gets done. . . . [See "The Curtis Report," above.]

The Right to Fly

But there is no technical solution to the basic conflicts of interests that traffic control in any form is bound to create.

Within the government, this conflict is between military and civil interests. In the air, however, the conflict is more complicated, for the airlines generally side with the military on every question of air control. Both are committed to all-weather flying, and find the burden of positive control in fair weather easy to bear. Both want to fly planes that are too fast for see-and-be-seen flying, but are big and expensive enough to justify the cost and weight of traffic-control equipment. Both use pilots who are professional in every sense.

Arrayed against the airlines and the military is "private aviation"—that amorphous group of fliers that range all the way from a college student in a rented Piper Cub to an entire board of directors on a plant-inspection trip in a two-engine transport. In the production of passenger-miles, of course, the airlines are dominant—last year they accounted for 19.8 billion. In sheer numbers of planes, however, private aviation is an impressive group. There are now 200,000 licensed private fliers, and the 60,000 private planes now flying outnumber by forty to one the 1,500 airline planes. In 1955 private planes flew 9.5 million hours—over three times the airline total. Business flying alone accounted for 4.3 million hours. (Nearly all of the nation's one hundred largest corporations operate one or more airplanes.) Then there is "agricultural" flying; the equivalent of one out of every twelve acres of farmland in the country has been treated in some manner from the air.

The problem is that private flying is already quite expensive, and any added burden in the form of a complicated positive-control traffic system would take most private fliers out of the air, good weather and bad. Few private fliers feel they can afford to meet the requirements of the present Instrument Flight regulations; quite aside from the cost of the extra equipment—$1,600 minimum for the lighter plane — Instrument Flight requires lengthy special training.

The private fliers feel they have a mission to preserve "freedom of the air" and so far they have proved very effective lobbyists. For years they have fought the military and the airlines to a standstill on the question of raising the Visual Flight minimums. To raise them would in effect increase the percentage of days governed by the positive control of the Instrument Flight Rules. The airlines and the military already dominate the air when visibility drops, and any attempt at extending Instrument Flight is interpreted by the private fliers as an attempt to extend this monopoly. Such a move is especially galling to private fliers at this time since it is the new fast airplanes, which few of them fly, that have tended to make Visual Flight dangerous.

The better to present their side, a number of private-aviation organizations . . . formed a "General Aviation Facilities Planning Group." The objective of the group is to

assemble convincing and irrefutable economic and technical data concerning our segment of aviation. Any air traffic control system which would upset the present favorable economic status of the private airplane would destroy our private air transportation industry, booming now as never before and really only getting started.

Compromise in the Air

Certainly, positive control will never take such a form as to put the private fliers out of the sky. There will have to be a compromise. The most likely one is a division of the air space into two segregated areas, each governed by a single traffic-control concept. One would be based on see-and-be-seen, the other on positive control in all weather. . . .

Private fliers are not the only ones who might lose out under positive air control. What, for example, will be the role of the professional pilot? Until recently, it had never been questioned, least of all by the airlines, that such decisions as where to end a flight and the choice of routes were the exclusive preserve of the pilot or his employer. Positive control could be the end of this independence on the part of pilots. More and more, they will be order takers, followers of decisions made on the ground, and highly likely to be made obsolete by automation. They do not face the prospect with equanimity.

Any move that transfers initiative from the pilot to air-traffic control personnel makes it all the more imperative that the government reach a decision as to its liability in accidents. Thus far the courts have ruled that so long as the controller is not negligent in his guidance, the liability stays with the pilot and the carrier. The new concept of positive control, however, requires that all aircraft in a controlled area obey the directions of the ground controllers, whether or not the pilots can see for themselves that an alternate decision would be better. This authority of the government should carry with it comparable responsibility, and new laws are needed to define the potential liability.

The Role of Radar

These conflicts of interests translate themselves eventually into questions of hardware. At the center of every argument is radar. It is at the center because it is the only device that allows the ground to know, theoretically at least, the location of every plane in the sky, without any help from the planes themselves.

Control schemes that emphasize radar, therefore, tend to discount the pilot as a decision maker; he isn't needed since the controller has all the information he requires. The reverse is also true; control schemes that make little use of radar generally leave much of the decision-making up to the pilot. This is only natural since the controller is dependent primarily on information received from the planes.

In the end, the question is just how dependable radar is—or can be. Whether radar can be improved to the pinpoint accuracy that thousands of flights can be entrusted to its perfect operation day after day is in serious doubt. A hard rainstorm can still clutter the screen, and even where spare equipment is on hand, there can be moments when an unfortunate coincidence of burned-out tubes can blank the image. Moreover, the newer-type planes fly at the very altitudes—helicopters near the ground, jetliners in the stratosphere—where line-of-sight radar finds it most difficult to locate them.

The alternative to using radar is to devise ways to "telemeter" —transmit — data on each plane's position directly from the plane's instruments to the ground. Traffic control as such has no responsibility for guiding aircraft to their destination, but most fast, high-flying craft must be equipped with fairly accurate navigation instruments anyway, and this information can be used directly by ground controllers in establishing the relative position of aircraft under their jurisdiction. (This is similar to what CAA controllers do today except that they receive their information only when the planes pass over widely spaced check points.)

But telemetering has its drawbacks, too. The aircraft itself has to find out where it is, and the equipment needed to do this adds weight and complexity in the very place where these are most burdensome. Moreover, the ease with which the telemetered information can be fed into a traffic-control computer is dependent on the uniformity of the data received. In other words, the system would truly be no better than the common denominator established by the aircraft with the poorest equipment. Finally, telemetering puts one more burden on overloaded communication channels. But at least the responsibility for equipment performance is widely distributed, and this is an asset no radar-based system can enjoy.

The chances are that the ultimate positive-control system will use combinations of radar and telemetering, and retain the advantages of each while overcoming most of the disadvantages.

II. THE CROWDED SKY

EDITOR'S INTRODUCTION

Cities have always arisen at the places most favorable to transport and trade. The earliest grew at the natural intersection of caravan trails. Later, with the development of water-borne commerce, cities were built around harbors that offered safe anchorage and ready access to the interior. And still later they flourished at the terminus of a railroad or the hub of many. Thus the location of most of America's cities was determined by the transportation facilities of yesterday—and their very growth has hampered the development of facilities for the transportation of tomorrow.

Good airports require vast areas of land—and vast areas of land are no longer obtainable within a reasonable distance of the great cities that support airways. They require elevated land, for elevated land offers fewer obstructions, better drainage, less fog, and more uniform winds. But elevated land, even if obtainable, is invariably too expensive and frequently inaccessible to the other systems of transportation that the airlines must supplement. And they require a peripheral business and residential community, for only such a community can provide the goods and services and amenities that the airport needs. But communities—because of noise, suspected danger, or the broad obstacle to growth presented by the facility itself—tend to grow away from airports rather than toward them. And when they do encompass an airport the airport is hemmed in.

Despite these innumerable and peculiar problems nearly seven thousand airports, civil and military, are operative in the United States and few large communities are without one. Most have been built in the past forty years. Prior to World War I commercial airfields were almost nonexistent and even the armed services had few worthy of the name. At the war's end in 1918 the Army had fifty, the Navy seventeen. When postwar demobilization forced the dismantling of many airfields, a cooperative plan was worked out between the Army and a few municipalities that were anxious to develop civilian facilities as replacements. This plan—the first governmental aid to civil air transport—was adopted in 1919 by thirty-two major cities and called for the Army Air Service and Army Corps of Engineers to provide plans and specifications, the Federal Government to provide hangars, the municipalities to provide land and maintenance. In 1924 the Air Service issued revised specifications, based on its own intervening experience, that remained basic for years. These specifications—simple, sound, and economical—proved to be an excellent foundation for future development, when followed. But many cities did not follow them. They built haphazardly on conveniently located pastures and the airports were inevitably outmoded by the swift development of the plane.

Many of these airports, hopelessly obsolete despite constant tinkering, are still in use. To replace them and develop others the Federal Government has expended over $300 million since passage of the enlightened Federal Air Transport Act of 1946. These funds, in accordance with the act, were matched by the municipalities receiving them and millions more will be forthcoming in the future as cities realize that adequate air transport is as vital to their commercial survival as adequate transport by rail or sea or road. All of these dollars, and more, will be needed, for the cost of modern airports is astronomical. The $9 million spent on Newark's new instrument runway would have built ten complete airports a generation ago, and New York's Idlewild has already cost $115 million, with $150 million more earmarked for improvement in the next ten years.

The airlines themselves cannot possibly build or maintain such facilities and nobody seriously thinks they should. Federal, state, and local grants to railroads—in land or money—ran into the billions during construction; trucks and buses operate on public roads, paying only a fraction of road maintenance costs; and congressional spending for the improvement of rivers and harbors has been so generous that the very name of such appropriation bills has become synonymous with the pork barrel. Airlines can, however, and will, improve the structure and operation of their own facilities at each airport. The dingy hangars and terminals, the long lines of cowed passengers waiting for a plane that never takes off, the gouging concessionaires, even the lack of creature comforts, are already becoming hallmarks of the past. They were perhaps inevitable in the swift and under-financed growth of air transportation, but they will be anachronisms in the modern airports of an established industry.

That industry is one of many facets, and it is with the lesser-known facets of commercial air transport that this section is mainly concerned. Some, like the "Flying Taxis" described by Norris Willatt, are recent arrivals. Others, like John A. Conway's air freighters and the feeder lines examined by the editors of *Business Week,* are already old by the comparatives of aviation. All, with the exception of "The Nonskeds" mourned by Robert Bendiner, are growing.

Three types of air traffic are discussed in this section. The first group of articles deals with passenger service, the second with freight, and the third with military transport.

LITTLE ONES THAT FEED THE BIG ONES [1]

The station manager for Allegheny Airlines at Bradford, Pennsylvania, is a man of many functions.

He may be found helping out in selling tickets, handling baggage, advising pilots on local air and ground traffic, making reservations, holding the fire extinguisher at engine start-up, or even gauging the weather.

These things must be done at all commercial airports, big or little. At little ones like Bradford, though, where the income is less, the number of employees has to be held down. So the station manager must lend a hand on a lot of tasks.

In a way, this situation is characteristic of the entire local service airline industry. It is filled with young management men who are working hard at a wide variety of jobs—many of which don't fall in the management category.

[1] From "For Feeder Airlines It's a Lot of Work for Low Pay." *Business Week.* p 32-6. December 29, 1956. Reprinted by permission of *Business Week,* a McGraw-Hill publication. Copyright 1956 by McGraw-Hill Publishing Company.

Despite this, the local airline industry can't make a profit on operations. All thirteen lines need government help in the form of subsidy beyond mail pay. In 1955, these subsidies ranged from a low of 14 per cent of total revenues in one case to a high of 67 per cent.

None of the thirteen has ever paid a cash dividend on its common stock, yet none has been able to build up a large financial reserve to meet the impending and essential reequipment program. It is generally agreed these carriers cannot make a profit with most of their present equipment. Yet, they'll have trouble financing new equipment unless they can show a profit.

The government doesn't want to go on paying subsidies to these airlines forever. At the same time it can't let them go out of existence. Too many communities, industries, and people have come to depend on them.

Vital Statistics

So the questions arise: For all the hard work that goes into them, what good does it do? Where are they going from here? And how do they propose to get there?

The local service airlines are scheduled carriers that have come into existence since World War II. They are Allegheny, Bonanza, Central, Frontier, Lake Central, Mohawk, North Central, Ozark, Piedmont, Southern, Southwest, Trans Texas, and West Coast.

Except for the Western Plains states, New England, and Florida, these airlines pretty well blanket the country. They serve 500 communities, of which about 270 receive their only air service from a local carrier.

The average hop of a local line is about 77 miles, and the average passenger journey is about 182 miles. In other words, these carriers are trying to do business in that phase of the airline industry where business is hardest to do. Less than 2 per cent of all common-carrier passengers fly on journeys of under 250 miles.

In the first nine months of 1956, according to the Air Transport Association, all the local airlines together carried 2,583,000 passengers, an increase of 19.6 per cent over the first nine months of 1955. By comparison, American Airlines, biggest of the domestic trunk lines, flew 5,856,721 passengers in the same period.

Through September, total revenues of local lines, including subsidies, amounted to $49,187,000—an increase of 16.8 per cent over the 1955 period. Nevertheless, the industry suffered a net loss of $410,000, compared with a net profit of $184,000 . . . [in 1955]. Operating expenses . . . [had] gone up 20 per cent in the year.

Community Interest

While the local service lines appear to be running ever faster without managing even to stand in the same place, they do a great deal for the economies of the many communities they serve. Take Bradford, for example. Located in the hills of northwestern Pennsylvania, it has a population of 17,000 that would be almost cut off were it not for the twenty flights a day provided by Allegheny Airlines. It has no direct rail passenger service and only infrequent buses.

Bradford is the headquarters of Zippo Manufacturing Company, maker of cigarette lighters. Since Allegheny started serving the town, Zippo has been able to extend its Christmas business about two weeks later than with surface shipments. During the first part of December, much of the production now goes by air.

Dresser Manufacturing Division of Dresser Industries is the town's biggest employer, with a payroll of 1,300 employees. Says a company official: "Because we depend on it for eighty per cent to 90 per cent of our transportation, we'd be lost without Allegheny."

And a spokesman for the new local Corning Glass plant, engaged in electronic component work, declares, "I don't think we would have moved into an area that didn't have commercial airline facilities."

Handicaps

In spite of the important part the local service airlines play in the transportation industry and the increasing number of passengers they haul, they continue to lose money largely because of obsolete planes, uneconomic routes, and archaic schedules.

All but three lines—Allegheny, Mohawk, and Southwest—use DC-3's exclusively. Though this plane was once the chief money-maker of the airlines, it's far from that now. While fares have held relatively steady over the years, the wages of everyone connected with operating and maintaining the plane have soared.

Since it's impossible to cram any more passengers into a DC-3, the plane can now earn less money even at the best of times. Right now, the profit for most lines comes only in filling the last four or five seats of a twenty-four-passenger plane. For local service carriers to fill those last seats is next to impossible. Because the airlines must schedule frequent stops, it's often necessary to leave seats empty for stations down the line.

If the first problem with the DC-3 is that it's too small, the second is that it's too slow. The cruising speed of a "3" is about 170 miles per hour. But when this plane is used in local service work, a lot of time is spent on aprons, runways, climbing, and letting down. The passenger's elapsed time on a flight turns out to be much longer than the listed crusing speed would indicate.

In other words, local service airlines are losing the chief advantage of the airplane—speed.

The third problem with the DC-3 is that it's too old. Douglas Aircraft Company has long since stopped making these planes or more important, spare parts for them. This means airlines still flying these twenty-year-old craft have to make parts themselves, have them custom-made elsewhere, or scavenge them from other DC-3's.

This can take weeks, while the plane isn't earning any money. And the part that's needed will cost far more than it used to.

Another reason why local airlines can't make a profit is their route structure.

The thinking behind the locals when they were first certificated by the Civil Aeronautics Board was that they would feed traffic to the major trunklines.

Under this concept, routes originally radiated from a central point to smaller communities. On inbound flights a plane would start practically empty, would fill up as it neared the trunkline city. On the outbound trip, it would gradually drop its load.

Then as now, the average load factor over the whole distance of such a flight was well below what it takes to make a profit.

In time, the locals sought and received extensions to more logical points for two-directional traffic. They were also awarded additional routes criss-crossing the old lines. These were to serve the surprising number of people who wished simply to go from one point to another within the local system.

As the local service carriers expanded in this fashion, they began to serve more and more of the smaller cities on trunkline routes. It is the contention of most local operators that the trunks skim off the cream of the business from these cities. This leaves the locals, who provide more flights but on slower schedules, unable to make a profit on the routes.

Certain costs in airline operations are fixed. It costs about the same, for example, to sell a passenger a ticket or handle his baggage whether he's going on a trip of two hundred miles or two thousand miles. But the return on the first passenger is one tenth that of the second. Local carriers insist that to make a profit they need longer routes.

Another major reason for losses, locals claim, is the schedules to which they must adhere. Being set up as feeders, they were originally obliged to make every stop on every flight. This quickly proved disastrous, since a smaller city was unable to generate the same traffic as a larger one.

Bit by bit, the CAB has allowed the locals "skip-stop" privileges, provided each town gets a certain amount of service. The local carriers insist they should be allowed to skip many more stops on many more flights. If they could, they might then sell the whole plane instead of holding seats for stations down the line. Faster express flights between major points, they claim, could generate more traffic and cut costs.

Costly Solutions

If the major problems are depressingly clear to the locals, so are the solutions. What's needed are bigger, faster planes, longer routes to more big cities, and fewer required stops along the way.

This pattern is just as clear and depressing to the trunks, for the big lines have a stake in it.

The original concept of feeder lines has largely disappeared. In its place, if the locals have their way, will grow an industry of regional trunklines. Obviously, a reasonable compromise must be worked out over the years to come.

In some cases, the major trunks would be willing to yield some of their less busy points to the regional lines—if they weren't convinced that by so doing they would be building up the smaller lines to the point where they would be real competition on major runs. Besides, lots of cities like the prestige of being on the "main line" and don't want to lose their trunkline even though it may provide only token service.

If many of the new route applications to CAB were approved, locals would not only invade the territory of the trunks but also invade each other. And the board believes that if locals are unable to compete without subsidy against trains, buses, and most particularly the private automobile, they are hardly strong enough to face competition from each other.

In the matter of a DC-3 replacement, at least one is finally on the way. It's a two-engine turboprop designed jointly by Fokker Aircraft Company in Europe and Fairchild Engine and Airplane Company here. The new plane, the F-27 Friendship, will have a cruising speed of 250 miles per hour, a range of 2,225 miles, will seat 40 passengers, and will be able to land and take off at most smaller airports. It should also be economical to fly and maintain.

The chief difficulty, however, is its price tag of $600,000, with radio and extras. A reequipment program based on airplanes costing such prices is not something that local service airlines, with their current financial state and uncertain future, can dive into lightly.

For the privately held lines, it may mean selling stock to the public; for those already publicly held, it may mean a major dilution of equity. For either, selling stock will not be easy, nor will borrowing money. Local service management is just about unanimous in thinking that the government must help finance new planes. [In September 1957 President Eisenhower signed a bill permitting the CAB to guarantee up to 90 per cent of the price of new planes bought by the twenty-three feeder, territorial, and helicopter lines provided they cannot get the loans elsewhere. There is a $5 million ceiling on loans to any one line.—Ed.]

Not all airlines are satisfied the F-27 is the final answer. So far, however, Frontier has ordered two and taken an option on four more. West Coast has ordered four and optioned four. Bonanza has ordered three and optioned three, and Piedmont—completely sold on the plane—has ordered twelve and optioned twelve.

For the future, there are two rays of hope. . . . [In 1956] CAB decided to investigate the local airline situation to determine whether or not there should be a new policy on earnings. This will give the industry a chance to present its case, particularly its equipment-financing needs. [In 1958 the CAB was still investigating, but an amendment to the Federal bankruptcy laws in 1957 let airlines set up equipment trusts similar to those used by railroads to buy rolling stock. In the event an airline goes bankrupt the lender gets first right to repossess, and resell, the equipment bought through the trusts. This makes borrowing for equipment purchases easier for the airlines, and lending safer. The amendment applies to all airlines but was pushed through Congress by the feeders.—Ed.] And for the longer term, the industry hopes that when the major trunks begin flying their huge jets, they will be willing to turn the intraregional business over to the locals.

THE NONSKEDS [2]

Back in 1938 Congress passed the Civil Aeronautics Act, sponsored by Senator Pat McCarran and nursed through a subcommittee by an obscure first-termer named Truman. The purpose was to spare the public, just then beginning to take to air travel, the long period of cutthroat competition that had marked the spread of rail travel in an earlier day. Protection of passengers from undue hazard, the need to stabilize an infant industry,

[2] From "The Rise and Fall of the Nonskeds," article by Robert Bendiner, contributing editor of *The Reporter,* and magazine writer. *The Reporter.* 16:29-34. May 30, 1957. Reprinted by permission.

and the requirement of a reserve transport fleet for national defense—all made it undesirable to leave the emergent airlines to the mercies of the Darwinian market place. At the same time, it was obvious that air transport was not a "natural monopoly" like gas or electricity and had to be allowed a measure of competition.

The Act therefore set up the Civil Aeronautics Board as a regulatory agency and provided for two types of carrier. Certificates were to be issued to the sixteen lines then flying passengers and mail, authorizing them to operate as regular "scheduled" airlines, and subsidies in the guise of flexible mail payments were to offset their deficits. In return they were obliged to meet standards of safety and convenience set up by the CAB and to fly routes that included marginal areas as well as the lush markets of big terminal cities. New lines were to be certified on a showing of "public convenience and necessity," provided the Board found them able and willing.

A second group, known as "fixed base operators," were to be granted exemptions from the regulations. They could make irregular trips, provide local taxi service, run charter flights, and perform other functions not related to regular public travel over a fixed route. Most of the trips were short ones in small planes, and at first the "fixed base operators" were of very little public significance. After the war, however, they suddenly became very significant indeed.

At a time when the demand for air service seemed unlimited, the government found itself with surplus transport planes on its hands while scores of trained pilots were pouring into civilian life eager to make use of their wartime experience. With the government's blessing—in fact with its financing—veterans and planes inevitably got together and nonsked air travel was launched.

If the CAB did not see that in the normal course of things some of these entrepreneurs hoped legitimately to develop into regular airlines, it was singularly lacking in imagination. It "must have realized," a Senate committee report was to state in 1953, "that these large transport-type aircraft would have to be

used in some sort of common-carrier route-type service." They
were hardly designed for crop dusting or for rushing Florida
oranges to Boston.

Among those who took their own future as public carriers
for granted were Stanley Weiss, an Army transport pilot who
had flown sixty-four trips over the Hump, and James Fischgrund,
a Navy lieutenant commander. For $15,000 down and an RFC
loan they bought two DC-3's and in 1946 set up business as
Standard Airlines. At about the same time Ross R. Hart and
Jack B. Lewin, both employees of Douglas Aircraft, raised the
small capital required to establish Viking Airlines, a similarly
modest enterprise. Their plan was to tap the vast potential
market of would-be air travelers who could not afford the luxury
prices of the regular lines. Their formula was to eliminate the
frills, especially free meals, to increase seating capacity, and to
fly as steadily as possible between points of heavy traffic. Cut-
rate coach flights were operated between Los Angeles and New
York for as much as $50 below the standard price. By 1948
Standard was in the black and had a fleet of seven DC-3's. Together the two lines had sewn up the lion's share of cut-rate
transcontinental traffic—$75 between Chicago and California and
$99 coast to coast.

Between 1947 and 1949, as Standard and Viking hauled in
the cash and the country in general enjoyed good times, the
"grandfather lines," overexpanded and evidently over-priced,
wallowed in their own exclusive depression. Inevitably they took
a jaundiced view of the upstarts even though their own deficits
were covered by the United States Government. W. A. Patterson, president of United Air Lines, subsequently put the case in
its now classic form to the Small Business Committee of the
Senate:

> The irregulars moved in to make the most of this [postwar] situa-
> tion, to fly anywhere at any time that loads were available. Thus began a
> cream-skimming operation whereby they would tap only the major mar-
> kets and leave the scheduled airlines to carry out their responsibility of
> serving all communities, large and small. Thus they began undercutting
> the scheduled airlines and each other. They had to file no tariffs; they
> had to meet no route qualifications; they could operate in and out of any

airport without prior crew familiarization procedures. Theirs was a free and easy business in which they had to answer to practically no one but themselves. The regulated, scheduled operators, with their obligations to the general public, to the government, to stockholders, and to employees, looked on with some amazement. . . .

"Strangulation by Regulation"

They looked also to the Civil Aeronautics Board—and there they found comfort. By defenders of the nonskeds the CAB is regarded as the greatest drag on aviation since gravity, but there is no doubt that the cut-rate fliers confronted it with a real dilemma. On the one hand it was directed by the Act to foster a sound and efficient air service without "unfair or destructive competitive practices," and on the other hand to encourage "competition to the extent necessary to assure the sound development" of the system. By certifying the nonskeds it could divest them of the advantages cited by Patterson, subjecting them to the same conditions as other regular lines, or it could keep them in their special status and squeeze them with regulations. Looking at the shaky financial state of the certificated carriers, perhaps with an eye on the subsidies for which it rightly felt it had a responsibility, and having no more boldness of vision than government bureaus generally have, the CAB moved toward regulating the brashness, if not the life, out of the nonskeds.

The process described by Senator John Sparkman as "strangulation by regulation" began in 1947. Blanket exemptions were withdrawn, and the nonskeds were required to apply for individual Letters of Registration as irregular carriers. Full reporting on rates, mergers, and other operating details were called for, and specific restrictions were laid down on the number of flights that could be made in a given period. Two years later the screws were tightened some more. The irregulars were prohibited from making arrangements, among themselves or with ticket agents, for interchange of passengers, or from rotating flights in such a way as to constitute a "collective air transportation service."

"Living up to those regulations was 100 per cent impossible, and the Board knew it," counsel . . . told the House Antitrust

subcommittee . . . [in 1956]. "That is why the Board adopted
the regulations." Senator Wayne Morse was even more specific:
"A traveler must know in advance when a plane is going to
depart, when it is going to arrive, where he can buy his ticket,
and from what place he can collect his baggage. These things
cannot be done if the operation is conducted on a tramp-steamer
basis." In any case, both Standard and Viking treated the rules
cavalierly. Both applied for certification and were turned down.
The CAB was more intent on strengthening the existing lines
than in adding to their headaches. By 1950 both lines had their
Letters of Registration revoked for flying too frequently, and
technically they went out of business.

Actually they merged, along with two other lines, into a complex corporate arrangement, and as North American Airlines
proceeded to do business in a highly profitable circumvention of
the CAB and its rules. Through a web of partnerships with an
interlocking directorate, they brought together the functions of
flying, leasing, ticket selling, and accounting. And by artful
shuffling of schedules they managed to furnish regular service
from Los Angeles to New York and New York to Miami without seriously transgressing the frequency limits for any one line.

If the regulars were irritated before, they were now outraged. "Interlopers," "pretenders," and "bogus specialists," the
nonskeds were called by Eastern Air Lines' president Eddie Rickenbacker—and these were among the more endearing names reserved for them. The Air Transport Association instructed its
legal department to get the CAB to forbid uncertificated operators even to use the word "airline" or "airway." When a passenger having to take two or more lines to complete a trip in-
quired about a North American connection, ticket clerks would
frequently express shock. On occasion they were heard to mur-
mur something about "safety," although North American had no
fatal accidents in its seven years of operation. Stanley Weiss of
North American testified before Representative Emanuel Celler's
Antitrust subcommittee that travel agents were warned by the
ATA to stop selling tickets for the nonskeds altogether or give
up their franchises from the major lines.

The Air-Coach Boom

In terms of revenue, North American was never remotely a threat to the certificated carriers, which did 96 per cent of the passenger trade. But it was a yardstick, and as such its influence has been as marked—and as unwelcome—in the business of air travel as TVA's in the field of electric power. Some trunkline executives dispute the North American group's claim to have pioneered in air-coach travel. Alexander G. Hardy, fiery vice-president of National Airlines, told me that his company had applied for permission to run a reduced-fare service from New York to Miami and had ordered coach planes before North American was even in the picture. Turned down by the CAB, which didn't think the idea financially sound, National took the matter to the courts but without success. What is more, Hardy said, the nonskeds appeared before the Board to oppose the move and then when it had been turned down went out themselves and flew at reduced rates.

Far from being the public's white knight, according to Hardy, "the nonskeds were gouging the public during the peak seasons." In the immediate postwar period, when demand far outran supply, they exacted as much as $100 for the New York-Miami run as against the standard first-class fare of $56.

Nevertheless, it was the nonskeds, especially Standard and Viking, that made a go of coach service. They were the first to increase the seating capacity of standard aircraft and to offer coach fares, not just for flights at inconvenient hours but on the basis of greater passenger load. Eventually forced to follow suit, the trunklines found themselves with a boom on their hands. In 1948, for example, Capital Airlines carried 1,002 passengers on its regular first-class run between Chicago and New York. In December of that year, the second month of its newly installed coach service, 3,072 made the trip at the reduced fare. Six years later, coaches accounted for fully a third of all domestic airline traffic and more than a half of the overseas. By 1960 all the big lines expect that more than half their passengers will travel by coach. Yet as late as 1949 United called such service "unsound" and American said air-coach travel had no part in their plans.

While the coach trade played a large part in getting the trunklines out of the red and, not so incidentally, off public subsidy, they found the "yardstick" no more tolerable on that account. The North American combine may have given the industry a shot in the arm, but if it was allowed to go on operating outside the regulations, as it patently was doing, what was the good of the CAB or the Act itself? If North American wanted to operate as an airline, let it apply for certification and abide by the rules of the game.

This attitude sounded reasonable, but there was one hitch. Since its creation in 1938, the CAB has yet to find a single applicant it considered worthy of certification as a regular passenger airline. Out of 164 applications, not one was deemed to have met the requirements of the Act. That 126 of these applications were withdrawn, or withered on the vine before a determination could be made, is in itself illuminating. . . . The net result is that with twenty times the traffic we have four fewer trunklines (because of mergers) than we had when the Act was passed.

Ambidextrous Appeals

The best the North American group could reasonably hope for was to forestall revocation of their Letters, and to this end they worked hard in Washington, covering both political sides of the street and ringing all the changes. Knowing how they stood with a majority of the Board, they concentrated elsewhere. Along with the other nonskeds, all of which were much smaller and less ambitious, they repeatedly and cogently presented their case before sympathetic committees on Capitol Hill. . . .

The appeal was essentially that of "the little man" at the mercy of monopoly, and it went well before the Senate's Select Committee on Small Business and Congressman Celler's Antitrust subcommittee in the House, both of which, unfortunately, had only peripheral jurisdiction in the field.

At the same time, the home office in California worked the other side of the street. It mailed out model letters and telegrams for sympathetic businessmen to send to the President, with copies for Vice President Nixon, appropriate congressmen, and Senators Knowland and Kuchel. . . .

For all its vigor and political ambidextrousness, however, the nonskeds' campaign was no match for the quiet pressure of the regulars. In the first place, the regulars had a strong technical case against the North American group, which, in spite of enforcement proceedings pending against it, merrily pursued its illegal way. It advertised itself blandly as "the fourth greatest airline in the United States" and the "largest and oldest air-coach system." Postcards were distributed at its ticket counters with the legend "Written aboard one of North American Airlines' luxurious four-engine Douglas DC-6B airliners," though at the time it was flying only DC-4's. Far from being reticent or indirect about scheduling flights contrary to regulations, it defiantly printed time-tables, adding only in very fine print at the bottom that these "samples of flight times are not representation that flights are made every day or with any specified regularity."

The regulars were every bit as alert to sentiment on the Hill as the nonskeds and played up to it from the start. In a letter to the heads of the certificated lines in 1948, Admiral Emory S. Land, then president of the Air Transport Association, laid down a public-relations program for combating the nonskeds' efforts to get air-freight business: "Finally, the most important part of this letter is that you personally contact one or more key men who, directly or indirectly, have this matter under consideration," his communication wound up. "The addresses of these key men are Capitol Hill and Commerce Building [where the CAB is located]. Nufced."

Another document produced at the Celler subcommittee hearings was a memorandum to the Public Relations Advisory Committee from John W. Thompson, an ATA official. Airlines were advised in this note to "get in touch" with a group of senators who had signed a petition in favor of slowing down CAB action against the nonskeds. It was to be pointed out to these legislators that unless the nonskeds were checked, "the areas which sent these gentlemen to Congress will be affected adversely as far as air passenger service, airmail, air parcel post is concerned." Once again, nufced. With the big airlines operating in every state if not in every congressional district, with their directors scattered in most major cities and generally men of considerable local importance, the impact of the regulars is very much greater than any that can be directed at congressmen by an isolated and comparatively small independent.

Friends in Court

It is with the CAB itself, however, that the "grandfather lines" have the vital advantage. The tendency is strong for members to identify themselves with the interests of the existing carriers, and to promote their financial health, if for no other reason than to keep them off government subsidy. Many of them conceive it to be their duty to build up these lines by adding to their routes, and a good case can be made that it is to the public's advantage to deal with a dozen expanded lines rather than with a network of small ones requiring intricate routing and frequent changes of plane.

Be that as it may, the degree of cooperation between the CAB and the giants is striking, and few uncooperative board members have ever been reappointed. . . . Given the feeling of the CAB's majority and the obvious violations of North American, no one was surprised when the CAB put out a "cease and desist" order in 1953. The surprise was that, largely because of the work of exceptionally able counsel, the line managed to continue for two more years, even adding another carrier to the combine, before the Board in July 1955 finally revoked its various Letters of Registration for "knowing and willful" violation of the Act. Even after that blow, the group continued operations, though somewhat limpingly, pending final adjudication in the courts.

Sympathy for the Trans American group is neither easy nor relevant. [The CAB proceeding was started in 1953 when the group was known as North American Airlines. It embraced four non-scheduled lines: Twentieth Century, Trans National, Trans American, and Hemisphere. The CAB's action became effective in June 1957 when the Supreme Court refused to review a United States Court of Appeals decision upholding the Board.— Ed.] Its stoutest defenders concede the violations. One, a senator, says bluntly that "it brought on its own demise," and another suggests that to have granted the certificate would have been "like giving a bootlegger a liquor license after Prohibition on the ground that he had proved his efficiency." . . .

In a financial way, moreover, the position of these particular "small businessmen," however wronged, will hardly draw tears. According to their counsel, each of the four partners drew $111,835 in 1954 and $101,726 in 1955, exclusive of their salaries of $2,000 a month. Net profit after taxes in the latter year amounted to $835,994. Even the pending collapse of their enterprise was used to turn a handsome profit. The line's five DC-6B's have been leased for five years to Eastern for between $35,000 and $40,000 a month per plane, for a total of $12 million. Since they are reliably reported to have cost around $7.5 million, the partners can forget all about flying and still split a profit of $4.5 million, not counting depreciation, on this leasing coup alone.

The financial fortunes of the partners, however interesting, have no bearing of course on the larger issue. "This was the last effort to crack the CAB policy against letting new trunklines into the business," I was told at Trans American, "and like 162 efforts before it, it failed." While this may be putting the case too strongly, the fact is that almost all the remaining nonskeds are concerned exclusively with military contracts and the few that are not are so small as to preclude ambition. There are . . . [a number of] certificated "feeder lines," which operate locally, but they are well subsidized even now and their expansion is not regarded as economically feasible. Yet except by operating profitably as a nonsked, how is any line to demonstrate the fitness and ability required for certification under the Act?

Is the door really closed to new lines? The CAB denies it, as it must, but one of its former chairmen says, "The answer probably is 'Yes.'" Nor does the prospect bother him. "Freedom of access in this field is ridiculous," he explains; "the Act never contemplated it." But the record of congressional debate seems to show otherwise. The Small Business Committee's report found it "filled with repeated assurances that the door would still be open to new companies."

It is true that the CAB has been steadily cutting the smaller trunklines into routes hitherto reserved for the Big Four, and in this process there is still room for competition. It is a competition, let it be admitted, unknown to the giant lines of other countries, but nevertheless it is competition among a select few, each satisfied with the status quo as soon as he has an adequate piece of the pie. If the pie has been greatly enlarged by expanded coach service—all the domestic trunklines are now off subsidy—the Big Twelve who will share it have North American to thank for prodding them into the low-fare market. In the nature of things, of course, they can no more be expected to shed a tear at the wake of the nonskeds than North American can be credited with high social purpose. A vice president of National Airlines, a small regular that has to contend with the giants above it while fighting the nonskeds beneath it, pretty well summed up the code of the trade. "No one in any business favors monopoly," he remarked, "until he's got one."

FLYING TAXIS [3]

A postwar baby, the air taxi business is growing up rapidly. Aerial hacking didn't get under way until 1946 when a few ex-Air Force pilots began renting out planes on an irregular charter basis. And it was only a scant four years ago that the major airlines recognized and agreed to cooperate with the new medium of transportation. This recognition was accorded on condition that the air taxi companies would meet certain standards with respect to regularity of service, reservations, insurance and liability. At the time of the agreement, the principal operators combined to set up the National Air Taxi Conference to administer such standards. Some one hundred firms are now Conference members, and others are being added all the time.

Thus, all over the country—but mainly in the major population areas of the East and Middle West—small planes are standing by, often on a twenty-four-hour basis, to answer calls for any kind of trip. Once airborne, they maintain the same kind of

[3] By Norris Willatt, associate editor of *Barron's*. *Barron's*. 35:13-14. September 12, 1955. Reprinted by permission.

two-way radio connection with base as ground taxis, so that they can be switched or redirected to pick up additional fares. The pilots wear a distinctive uniform, like a cabby, and the service nation-wide has adopted the emblem of a flying kangaroo—"for short hops."

So far, entry into this new and expanding business has been possible with a relatively limited outlay. In 1953, the National Aviation Trades Association conducted a survey that produced data on all businesses which included air taxi service as one source of revenue. The survey revealed that the average investment in aircraft and equipment—usually two or three planes and rarely more than six—was about $33,000. Payroll costs apparently need not be high, since the survey also showed that only 5 per cent of the operators employed more than thirty persons, while 70 per cent employed seven or fewer.

Most operations, as well, have been developed in situations where it was relatively simple to graft an air taxi service onto some existing enterprise. The owner of a local airport who already had some light planes for instructing students could easily, and at small cost, either divert some of them to taxi service, or add to his fleet. A distributor of light planes who was also in a position to lease hangar space at an airstrip could get his equipment at the usual discount.

For anyone moving into the air taxi business from scratch, however, the initial investment would be very much greater. He would have to acquire an airstrip with adjoining hangar, office building and passenger waiting room, with toilets, required of all operations that want National Air Taxi Conference recognition. Above all, he would have to have the know-how that comes only from experience with flying and fliers. For these reasons, then, the entrepreneur is most likely to enter the field by acquiring an interest in some established, growing enterprise.

Such operations are many and varied, and some are pretty specialized. For example, the Cape and Islands Flight Service, of Massachusetts, is mainly engaged in ferrying vacationists and commuting businessmen between Nantucket and adjoining islands and the mainland. The Southern Flight Service, Inc., operating out of Charlotte, N.C., primarily carries passengers to connect with major airline stops in the state. Guy Miller, who operates the Miller Aviation Center at the Allegheny County Airport, derives a large part of his revenue from a shuttle service between that terminal and the new Greater Pittsburgh Airport. Jess Kimball, who owns the Spa Flying Service operating out of the Memorial Field in Hot Springs National Park, Arkansas, does a large part of his total business making connections for spa visitors with the Delta-Chicago and Southern flights out of Little Rock.

Some aerial cab firms are based at local municipal airports, such as the Idaho Air Service, at Boise; the Sky-Taxi service, of Tulsa; the Hawthorne Flying Service, of Charleston, S.C.; and Aircraft-co, of Wichita, Kansas. It is not surprising, then, that of a total of some 44,000 passengers carried by members of the National Conference in the period between January and September 1954, about 16 per cent were either delivered to or from airline connections. The airlines also look favorably on the very junior service as an outlet for any overflow of passengers, and for enabling customers to make short emergency flights where the major carriers do not go.

Like the ground taxi service, some airborne cabbies have a zone system of fares. In the New York City area, for example, nine zones have been established, each twenty-five miles wide. Fares begin at a minimum of $15 for the innermost zone, and rise to a maximum of $180 at the 225-mile radius. Beyond this, a straight rate per aircraft mile applies. In the past the rate has generally worked out at between 15 and 20 cents a mile on smaller planes, such as Beech Bonanzas, Piper Cubs and Pacers and Cessna 140's to 180's, seating one to three passengers. More recently, some operators have been adding larger planes, such as Piper Apaches, Beech Twin Bonanzas and Cessna 310's, which carry five or six passengers. For these, the rates are 35 cents a mile and up. All passengers are charged round trip fares, incidentally, even if they travel only one way. On the other hand, rates are usually per plane, so that the larger the party, the smaller the individual cost.

Because of the short time that air taxis have been around on an organized basis, and the smallness of the individual operation, very little financial data is available on this type of business. What there is, however, suggests that it can be profitable, and that it is likely to grow more so. One owner who is prepared to divulge his operational breakdown is William J. Lotzer, president and major stockholder of Gran-Aire, Inc., at the Curtiss-Wright Airport, Milwaukee. Mr. Lotzer converted a charter service started in 1946 into a regular air taxi business in 1951. His original equipment was a Cessna 170, which cost him $9,000. Since then he has added a Cessna 195 and a Cessna twin-engine T-50, for an additional investment of $35,000. He has also made arrangements to lease a DC-3 from Purdue University for larger parties.

Mr. Lotzer reports that while air taxi is only part of his overall operations, it is a highly profitable part. Net profit on his investment of $44,000 has totaled $16,000 over a three-year period. . . . All these profits have been plowed back for expansion, additional facilities, and promotion. The company is planning to open an office at General Mitchell Field, the terminal point of Milwaukee, and to expand to Maitland Field there, if the latter remains open. Eventually, a Cessna 310 will be added to the fleet, and—even more long-range—perhaps some helicopters.

Jess Kimball's Spa Flying Service in Arkansas was started in 1946 on the basis of two $400 loans from the Arkansas Trust Co. and the Arkansas National Bank. These were used to make down payments on two Luscombe 8-A two-seater planes. The turning point in this enterprise came when Tom Miller, vice president of Chicago & Southern Airlines, took an air taxi trip and subsequently suggested establishment of the shuttle service from Hot Springs to Little Rock. The Spa Flying Service now operates with four Cessnas. About 77 passengers are carried in an average month, although at the peak of the tourist season the total may go as high as 150.

Spa's original investment in equipment amounted to $8,000 and an additional $67,000 has since been laid out on equipment and facilities. Mr. Kimball, who is sole owner of the business, does not break down profits from all his operations, which include the training of students, sightseeing, survey and patrol and other charter work. But he estimates that 80 per cent of total gross income of $38,497 in 1954—that is, some $30,000—came from air taxi. No net figure is revealed, but expenses would appear to be low. The pilots, including the owner, are paid on a percentage-of-fares basis, and one girl handles the office routine.

Probably the largest, and certainly one of the most successful air taxi operations in the country, is that of Red Bank Airport. Because Red Bank is located close to the New York airline terminal hub, its little light planes may be seen daily approaching and leaving the runways at La Guardia or Idlewild, or nestling in the shadow of a DC-7. The Carey Transportation offices at the major airline terminals act as agent also for the air taxi service.

Walter Laudenslager, of Red Bank, added air taxi to his airport operation, hangar rental, light plane dealership and student training activities in 1951. In its first year, the air taxi service lost more than $8,000. It made about $8,000 the next year, however, and in 1953 profits climbed to $13,000. Last year, the net was around $12,000. Meanwhile, gross income has quadrupled, and equipment has expanded from two to eight aircraft. At first the boss was the only pilot, but now there are five on regular assignment—with four more on emergency call.

Operators in the air taxi business are expansion minded. The limited experience they have had, coupled with growing public awareness and acceptance of their service, has convinced them that there is room for both larger operations in existing territories, and for new, bigger or better services by air taxi in unexploited areas. The leaders in the young industry say they are ready to go anywhere, at any time, at the drop of a hat, and stay away as long as necessary. It is in this kind of aerial free-lancing, in fact, that they foresee the fattest future profits.

FLYING WINDMILLS [4]

In time, those who chronicle such things may well decide that the summer of 1957 marked a significant milestone in scheduled helicopter transportation. It was not only that industry's tenth

[4] From "The Quick and Nimble Carriers." *Bee-Hive* (United Aircraft Corporation). 32:2-15. Fall 1957. Reprinted by permission.

anniversary; it was also a period in which, probably more than ever before, the public saw clearly the helicopter's high potential as a commercial vehicle. Behind the advent of this recognition, however, lay years of spadework on the part of a fledgling helicopter airline industry whose four members—Los Angeles Airways, Chicago Helicopter Airways, New York Airways, and Sabena Belgian World Airlines—have zealously pioneered this newest advance in public transportation. . . .

Increasingly the helicopter is funneling more and more people to big metropolitan airports where they can connect with the major airlines. Joint fare plans are available which permit air travelers to use helicopters at reduced rates. . . . Each of the lines has set its own pace in establishing its pattern of growth. The problems of one of them are not necessarily common to the industry. The present passenger operations of New York Airways and Chicago Airways are geared mainly to handling a multi-airport situation which does not exist for Los Angeles Airways or Sabena. Both New York and Chicago are constantly shuttling people back and forth, not only between their downtown areas and the airports, but also between the airports themselves. In the case of New York, many travelers find their inbound trunkline flight landing at LaGuardia while their connecting outbound flight will be taking off from Idlewild. The same situation applies in Chicago between Midway and O'Hare Fields. Los Angeles Airways, however, has, in effect, a single huge commercial airport situation so it has thus far concerned itself with transporting passengers, mail, and express between many of the outlying towns which surround the city and Los Angeles International Airport. . . . The next logical step for LAA will be the development of intercity service or transportation between the downtown areas of large cities such as Los Angeles and its suburban communities.

Sabena's passenger helicopter operation, on the other hand, is designed to supplement the airline's transatlantic fixed-wing service between Brussels and New York. From Brussels, the airline's helicopter network covers about 900 route miles, the longest being the Brussels-Paris run of 189 miles which takes about one hour and fifty-five minutes. Sabena's fleet of eight Sikorsky

S-58 helicopters serves twelve cities in Belgium, West Germany, Holland, and France. The line is proud of its center-to-center service between large cities. Often it is faster than that offered by fixed-wing carriers when surface travel time between downtown areas and airports is considered. For instance, Sabena's helicopters will consistently make better over-all time between Paris and Brussels than the line's airplanes which also serve the two cities. The popularity of this kind of service was clearly demonstrated last summer when Sabena, the first international helicopter passenger line, carried its one hundred thousandth passenger.

Observing the rule that it is better to learn to walk before you run, each of the four operators started by first carrying mail by helicopter and gradually worked up to where their individual managements decided they were ready to start transporting passengers. Mail, however, remains as an important part of helicopter transportation. Scores of suburban communities depend on helicopters for their airmail service today. The helicopter airlines, in practice, provide a service which many of these communities only had in theory before. . . .

The Flush of Youth

Most of the people who work for the helicopter airlines have that sparkling enthusiasm which accompanies intense interest. They know they are in on the ground floor of an industry with a bright outlook and the majority are willing to make that extra effort which insures success. As one young executive put it recently, "You never heard of a pioneer who worked a forty-hour week, did you?"

The pilots of the industry meet the same rigid physical requirements as do other scheduled airline pilots. They are in the same general pay brackets as those who work for local airlines. As combat pilots, many of them flew helicopters in Korea where the machine's matchless versatility was first brought sharply into focus. They share the spirit of fellowship that is the universal trademark of men who fly for a living. There, in many ways, however, the similarity ends. The average helicopter pilot follows about the same working schedule as most of his prosaically employed neighbors. He may on occasion go to work a little earlier if he has an early flight or, if he is with a line that operates around the clock, he may even work the night shift. . . . The helicopter pilot seldom gets the opportunity to know the people he carries as does his local service and trunkline counterpart. His cockpit connects with the passenger cabin only by the aircraft's intercommunication system which permits passengers to talk to the pilots. Moreover, the average flight of the three United States lines is only ten or twelve minutes while Sabena's is about thirty minutes. The average helicopter pilot's rotary-wing experience is about 750 hours, although some may argue that this seems a little high. The majority have fixed-wing experience. . . .

Many of those people being introduced to rotary-wing flight by the four present helicopter carriers have returned to their home cities and asked, "When are we going to get this service?" In the United States alone the Civil Aeronautics Board has about sixty applications pending for scheduled helicopter service in every corner of the nation. The Civil Aeronautics Board is the Federal agency which oversees the financial help the government is presently giving to the helicopter airlines. The Federal Government traditionally has helped all public transport industries get started in this country. The leaders of the helicopter airline industry are anxiously looking forward to the day, however, when their companies are free of subsidy. . . .

Robert L. Cummings, Jr., the president of New York Airways, reports that . . . in July [1957] alone his line carried 9,100 passengers, an impressive figure for a young airline when you remember that in 1926 the eight scheduled air carriers then existing in this country carried a total of 5,782 passengers for the entire year. During July, New York Airways also carried 60,000 pounds of freight, 122,000 pounds of express, and 250,000 pounds of mail with its fleet of five S-55's, three S-58's, and one Bell 47. Statistics like these emphasize Cummings' optimism in which he foresees subsidy-free helicopters in five years, operating daily routes, for instance, from downtown New Haven to downtown Philadelphia. While the bulk of New York Airways' pas-

sengers are inter-airport traffic, the line also runs regular passenger
service to White Plains, New York; Stamford, Connecticut, and
Teterboro, New Jersey. Mail and cargo flights serve Norwalk
and Bridgeport, Connecticut, and passenger service will be added
as soon as suitable heliports are available. . . .

New Helicopters, New Horizons

Probably more than anything else, the helicopter airline
people are anxiously looking forward to the introduction of the
large, twin-engined, gas-turbine-powered helicopter. One already
under development at Sikorsky is expected to be in operation
about 1960 or 1961. Designs are well past the drawing board
stage, and Sikorsky-designed, gas-turbine-powered helicopters
have already been test-flown. The gas turbine, with its higher
power and lower weight, has opened up new possibilities in
helicopter engineering. Studies indicate that as size goes up,
costs will come down. In the case of a twenty-passenger helicopter with two turbine engines, costs may drop as low as nine
cents or less for direct per-passenger-mile of operation. This is
well below today's piston-powered seven- to twelve-passenger
helicopters.

One evening late last summer, a Chicago cab driver reduced
to simple, meaningful English all the charts and statistics which
can be offered to prove out the helicopter's future. Pulling out
from in front of the Midway Airport terminal building, he
leaned over his cab's steering wheel to catch a better look at an
incoming helicopter.

"It's wonderful what's been done in the past twenty years,"
he said, "even if you just take air transportation. In the cities
alone, where traffic really chokes things up, these helicopters are
the coming thing."

FARES: UP OR DOWN? [5]

The airlines are pushing hard for a fare increase. [In a
hearing that opened in 1957 before the Civil Aeronautics Board]

[5] From "Air Fare Hearing to Open," article by Paul J. C. Friedlander, resort
and travel editor of the New York *Times*. New York *Times*. p X21. November 17.
1957. Reprinted by permission.

they argue that unless they get more money from the passengers they will begin to go broke very soon, will be unable to pay for new jets already on order, will be unable to raise cash through loans, equipment bonds or stock issues, and will have to go back on government subsidy or into bankruptcy or consolidation.

Capital Airlines, trapped by orders for new jet and turbo-prop planes, for which it is unable to pay or borrow money, has already asked the CAB to restore its mail subsidy to keep it afloat. Presidents of other airlines, presenting their cases in the friendly atmosphere of business meetings, have threatened to cancel jet orders and deny the customers the pleasures of jet flight unless they get increases ranging up to 15 per cent.

The airlines' big pitch will be that while domestic air fares have not increased substantially since 1938, all other services, costs, wages, etc., have risen sharply, and the airlines are, therefore, paying more for all their essential supplies, wages and equipment, without a comparable rise in their income. . . .

However, the airlines do not recognize that theirs is a new service, that in 1938 they were offering only luxury transportation for the wealthy few and that their fares were, therefore, at a peak. A peak, incidentally, that was not predicated on a mass market, high frequency of equipment use, high-density seating and thus a strong increase in numbers of passengers and revenue passenger miles.

Originally they were amortizing the cost of new planes over six or seven years; experience has shown their practical life to be double or triple that, and the jets are going to be amortized over periods close to fifteen years. This is the equivalent of taking a fifteen-year rather than a six-year mortgage, with lower monthly payments required for the longer loan, the result being more operating cash left in the airlines' tills. That is one of their big complaints, that the spread between operating costs and revenues is growing so thin that they soon will have no cash (or profit) left over to plow back into the business or to share with stock-holders. . . .

The airlines' testimony will attempt to show that the rise in their volume is in the lower tourist-fare trade which is not as profitable to them as first-class, or as they would like it to be. In the year ended June 30, 1957, coach passengers represented

37.6 per cent of the business; first class, including reduced-rate family plan, 62.4 per cent. However, airline officials rarely recall that they were forced into the air-coach service, especially on the transcontinental runs, by competition from the nonscheduled lines, which cut the rate down to $88 New York-Los Angeles.

The scheduled lines drove the nonscheduled ones out of business by adopting the $88 fare, which they had claimed was unreasonable and unsound, and by enlisting CAB official action in court to run the nonskeds off the airways. At $88, the airlines built up a brisk tourist trade across the country and managed to show some pretty handsome profits until recently. . . .

The nonskeds also forced the scheduled carriers to bring the New York-Florida run, one of the busiest and most profitable in the world, down to the $44 coach level. In season both the coaches and first-class planes are jammed full.

The airlines plan to argue further that they are offering brisk competition to each other, fighting to provide bigger, better, faster planes, more non-stop service, better cabin service, fancier meals and drinks, better ground service.

This, of course, is not price competition as envisioned in the free enterprise business system. The planes are almost identical, so are the stewardesses and the counter attendants. And the quality of service in all the airlines from the reservation desks through to the information clerks is notoriously variable, from good to downright bad, and, when weather and traffic both get heavy, abusive of the passenger's rights as a paying customer.

A passenger from Washington to New York, for example, has the competitive choice between flying a DC-6, a twin-engine Convair, a twin-engine Martin, a standard Constellation or a big new Super-C or Super-G Connie, or a DC-7; he also has a competitive choice of landing at Newark, La Guardia or International Airport. But whatever line or flight he gets, he pays the same price.

He can argue that through his local, state and Federal taxes he is helping support the air carriers by providing airports for them (for which they pay rent and landing fees), and by providing Civil Aeronautics Administration airport control towers, towermen, electronic landing systems, electronic airways and safety controls along these highways in the sky. Railroaders can join the argument with their thesis that they own and maintain and pay taxes on their own rights of way, trackage, etc. But the vast land grants given the railroads in their early days must not be forgotten now. Trucks use the highways free except for license fees and gasoline and oil taxes, but the airlines pay the taxes also.

All of which goes to prove that the rate case . . . is going to be one of the most complicated studies of its kind. . . . For who . . . can determine the value, in the fare to be charged the peacetime passenger, of the existence of a commercial air fleet . . . that can be converted overnight into an invaluable branch of an Air Force mobilizing for war? [On October 14, 1958, the CAB authorized a temporary increase (effective until July 31, 1959) in the round-trip and family-plan fares of the major airlines.—Ed.]

FREIGHT AND THE FUTURE [6]

Any plane can carry some kinds of cargo some distance at a profit, sometimes. The development of American commercial air freight has been a decade's struggle between that evident fact and its inexorable corollary: self-supporting air freight requires a plane conceived, designed, and built as a freighter.

The paradox that we already have a vigorous commercial air freight, expanding in every dimension of tons, dollars, and miles, despite the imperfection of its tools, derives from the artificial incubation of the war.

The first scheduled all-freight cargo liner took off in 1943. Like its sisters, then bulging with military cargo, that converted passenger plane was far from perfect for its purpose. . . .

War had demonstrated what wings would lift. To the jungle, the Arctic, and the five continents had flown very nearly whatever was wanted—incredible amounts, shapes, and items of it in planes that were not built to carry freight. They had to carry it. The GI who saw cases of soft drinks as well as bulldozers trundled down the ramps of ATC [Air Transport Command] might well have said with Lincoln Steffens: "I have seen the future and it works."

[6] From "Freighters of the Future" by Robert Gross, president of Lockheed Aircraft Company, and William Wister Haines, novelist and playwright. *Atlantic Monthly.* 192:37-41. August 1953. Reprinted by permission.

It did work—miracles of physical accomplishment. The fiscal reckoning, like the planes, terminals, and cargoes themselves, was governmental. The taxpayer footed the bill.

Yet so alluring was that preview of possibility that since the war eighty-six companies, mostly composed of former GI's, have entered the air freight business. Four of them survive. There were many factors in these failures. The primary one was the unsuitability of available planes for commercial cargo carrying.

Only now, ten years after the first converted passenger liner stripped out its seats, is the true freight plane progressing from mock-up to manufacture. Had this plane been available to the vision and energy of the eighty-six pioneers, their incidence of failure would have been very different. It took their experience and failures to shape this plane.

The air freight problem is only in part an adjustment of plane, terminal, and cargo. The most significant factor in air freight, as in everything to do with aviation, can be called political; it is man's ineradicable preoccupation with weapons.

The wing is a weapon. Realization that a nation with inferior wings might cease to be a nation put the American government, like all others, into aviation. Air power needs deep roots to defend its secondary right to make the wing a tool.

Since the magnitude of the need exceeded the scope of private capital, public interest had to underwrite some of the risk. Subsidy by airmail contract for the development of privately owned passenger lines was an expedient that fitted the capabilities of the early planes. It gave the taxpayer some immediate return on the industry he needed. It nourished aviation's growth toward self-support.

In pursuit of this concept Congress authorized the Civil Aeronautics Board to grant franchises (and airmail contracts) to private companies which could show that their projected operations between designated terminals were, in the words of the act, "in the public necessity and convenience." Those words were a restraint against suicidal competition on foreseeably lucrative routes. They were also an invitation to private brains, energy, and capital; to free enterprise; in a word, to profit.

The limitations of the planes of the time pointed these arrangements toward mail and passenger traffic. Both franchises and subsidies were revocable. The subsidies would terminate after satisfactory development of passenger revenue. They looked to the day when passengers would carry the mail instead of riding on it. But that day had to wait for better planes.

Even then perspective outlined a secondary objective of incalculable proportions. Long experience had shown the world of surface transportation, as air calls the wheel and keel carriers, that passenger revenue is only about one fifth of the total, or one quarter of the returns for hauling freight.

Now if passengers could be expected ultimately to carry the airlines, as upon sober projection they were, the question was not so much what air freight would carry as what it would not.

So it looked to the founders of the eighty-six companies. They had already seen wings lift almost every imaginable article of man's making. They had learned their trade in wartime air transport. Could monetary accounting be worse than reckoning in blood? No one knew better than they that the perfect, even the appropriate, plane for freight was not at hand. Who ever began anything with a perfect tool? They would try it.

To report that eighty-two of them failed is to report only one side of the experiment. The other side is that, largely by their efforts, our national air freight . . . skyrocketed from an annual lift of roughly 40 million ton-miles in 1946 to roughly 250 million in 1952.

Of these totals the passenger lines carried a proportion that increased as the independent freighters dropped out. They will play a prodigious part in the expansion that is expected to reach a billion ton-miles for 1959. Other projections set that same year as the one in which freight, measured in both weight and dollar revenue, will overtake passenger traffic.

Effects of World War II

The war which incubated air freight also retarded its adjustment to the commercial problems of peacetime. War stripped our airlines of their passenger planes when demand was soaring.

V-J Day found aircraft manufacture facing an unprecedented backlog of orders for replacement, expansion, and improvement of passenger equipment.

In addition to their moral claims, the old customers were solvent. Many had already cut the umbilical cord of subsidy. New planes would enable others to do so. Government guarantee still remained available to need. The manufacturer, pondering his duty to stockholders, employees, old customers, and country, knew that subsidy as well as solvency underwrote passenger plane orders.

In the field of the freighter the gargantuan subsidy of the war itself worked oppositely. The aviation boneyards were cluttered with war surplus planes. Economical or not, they would skim the cream off potential air cargo. The prices at which these planes were resold to the multiplying freight carriers constituted an indirect subsidy which acted against the manufacture of true freighters. . . .

The cut in government appropriations after World War II left the plane manufacturer almost alone to confront the staggering costs of new plane development. Especially in freighters, his failing prospective customers could not even share in the cost of a thorough study of their needs. Logic might insist that the government would also need a true freighter for military cargo. At the time, appropriations were inadequate to the grim race for improved combat types.

Against this background the plane manufacturer began, at his own expense, the study of commercial air freight. For he, too, remembered the four to one ratio of freight and passengers in other transportation. If subsidy would not lead to that, innovation must. Cargo would have to lift commercial freight as truly as the plane lifted cargo.

Queen cargo would never do it. Orchids—indeed all flowers —are ideal air freight. Their weight-value ratio, their perishability, the climate factor that puts optimum production so far from metropolitan demand—these are prime characteristics. The plane carries flowers at a profit. The question was what kind of plane flowers would carry.

Some items of air cargo are economical for all concerned at a dollar a ton-mile. But the eighty-two companies were failing in the 20 to 10 cents per ton-mile bracket. Savage rate wars did swell the casualty list; the real problem was volume to bear irreducible fixed costs.

The rate-volume ration in air freight is not a flight of steps. It is a pyramid of steps; every descent broadens the base. Cargo that cannot pay, say, 16 cents per ton-mile will literally leap into the air at 15 cents.

Measuring this pyramid by experience, analogy, and projection, surveying that ever-broadening base against his own long struggles with gravity and inertia, the plane manufacturer finally pronounced his dictum. His studies placed the highest possible base for a self-supporting air freight industry at about 4 cents a ton-mile.

To many an operator these words seemed the requiem of the air freight dream. They appeared to ignore the rising totals of tonnage then traveling between 20 and 10 cents.

The more thoughtful knew better. The 20 to 10 rates were already bankrupting most freighters. And they had been able to offer them only in war surplus planes, irreplaceable at the prices which put them into freight. Very few had ever touched the 9-cent level, even under optimum conditions. No converted passenger plane could ever get down to 4-cent operation.

True it all was, but still not final. For, accepting his own logic, and still at his own expense, the manufacturer had extended his study to outline the totally new plane that would carry 4-cent cargo—the first true freighter.

The differences between the revolutionary four-center and even the most efficient of previous conversions make a large library of blueprints. The luxury liner's solicitude for leg room was out. The four-center's pay load would be solid bulk. This meant a stronger floor to support it, a new frame to support the floor, new power to lift it all.

It is propeller clearance that keeps luxury liner doors up so many steps. But those steps so dear to photogenic actresses and ambassadors make hoisting charges for freight. Up went wings and engines above the airframe and down came side doors to truck bed level. Still the four-center must be able to swallow a loaded truck. Ingenious ventral doors permit it to drive straight in.

Even plumbing had to be reconsidered. Livestock of all kinds was already an important item of 10- to 20-cent air freight. The four-center had to be prepared for floods Noah never mentioned.

Gross weight, net lift, speed, altitude, range, takeoff and landing runs, length and strength of runways—these and the other variables of aerodynamics all had to be refitted to the new constant of 4-cent cargo.

Speed is the primary attraction of air freight, but in aerodynamics as in economics you do not get something for nothing. You buy speed not only with fuel but with frame limitation.

Is the shaving of a few hours for fresh sea food more valuable than space for air-minded furniture? Would fruit and vegetables freeze in the stratospheric speedways that are ideal for the distribution of new dress styles? Altitude and range are functions of speed as well as of space. Would the plane that trades Texas produce for Chicago mail orders deliver mining machinery over the Andes or drilling bits to Abadan?

One by one the variables had been fitted to the invisible framework of the 4 cents on every blueprint. One by one they took their places in another equation which, in effect, said finally that 4 cents equal $40 million. That would be the cost of the prototype. Line production at the rate of fifty planes a year might hope for a delivery price between $1.5 and $2 million dollars apiece.

This was very long arithmetic for an industry short of everything but guts. The impasse was broken by an older need than commercial air freight. The wing was still a weapon and modern war had brought the closest fusion yet between weapon and tool. The urgencies which originated military air transport had finally demonstrated the limitations of the converted planes that began it. In uniform as in mufti, the cargo problem had outgrown hand-me-downs.

When the services requested competitive bids for the best conceivable air transport, three manufacturers submitted plans. With the selection of the winner the 4-cent freighter was assured. . . .

The Air Freight Terminal

The farthest flights of engineering fancy, like the airframes that enclose them, must come to ground in terminals. Too many of our existing airports are already inadequate. They reflect a complacent approval of the divine wisdom which gave the passenger two legs. Freight will not walk. . . .

Integral in the manufacturer's study of the 4-cent plane are plans for its terminal needs. Some can be answered within existing airports. Some will require new ones. All terminals must have facilities now available in very few. Blueprints as well as advice for the necessary roads, docks, refrigerators, warehouses, rolling bridges, conveyors, and servicing shops are waiting. . . .

The freight terminals in the airports of both present and future will profoundly influence the impact of 4-cent air freight upon our industrial geography. Better terminals might have meant survival for some carriers who perished in the 20- to 10-cent bracket. The 4-cent plane will reverse the situation. Goods, service, and labor are going to shift to it. . . .

In the long run, cargo, through appropriate charges, will pay for adequate terminals. This does not build them now. The community, region, and industry which wait to see it pay should ask themselves not only when but where it is going to pay.

America is dotted with once-proud cities decaying on the shores adequate to nineteenth-century transportation. Many a village withers a few miles from the steel rails it misjudged. Los Angeles and Houston, on the other hand, reached imperiously for harbors. Denver built the Moffat Tunnel.

Past terminal problems have been chiefly municipal. The early freighters have had to stick to existing runways. The compasses of the 4-cent plane, however, are set to cargo itself—mercantile, industrial, and agricultural. The 4-cent terminal must be regional.

Helicopters have already proved their practicability as feeders for mail and military freight. Parachuting of commercial freight is as possible as parachuting military supplies. In commercial practice the pulling of the rip cord creates that economic anomaly, an empty plane. But if the plane is near the end of an economic run, near a terminal waiting with profitable reload, the parachute may revolutionize both distribution costs and industrial real-estate values. . . .

Time Is Money

For the wing as a weapon, air cargo was whatever had to be moved. . . .

For the wing as a tool, cargo is what is economic. An engine part worth $40 in New York undergoes an economic metamorphosis when a break in its counterpart stalls a steamship worth $4500 a day in Bombay. A box of windshield wipers in Detroit may be worth far more than their weight in gold to a Los Angeles auto assembler whose lines and storage yard are clogged for want of them. On the line those wipers are applied for a few cents apiece. Follow-up attachment by embarrassed dealers may cost several dollars.

These needs arise from emergency. So, beginning with war itself, does almost all air freight. But wars end. Commercial freight, first airborne in emergency, usually proceeds, through what might be called "emergenesis," into practice. Having learned the succoring power of wings, that ship in Bombay can chart a more profitable return route, still within their reach. The auto assembler can start his lines on smaller reserves, or even without some items, now only hours away in Detroit.

Emergencies teach, but only if someone is around to learn. It was the eighty-six companies which took the hard lessons through emergenesis. It was their desperation to find cargo for empty planes and inexorable gasoline cost which disclosed the broadening base of the rate-volume pyramid. Their struggle demonstrated something far more significant than the firm foundations of the 4-cent level. . . .

Outside San Antonio, before 1946, an okra grower supplied his accessible market with three acres of planting. Perishability limited him to neighborhood demand. Today he plants fifty acres; Wednesday's picking is Thursday's dinner in Detroit and Cleveland.

Those forty-seven acres of okra are new wealth in the world, created by an air freighter's need, and availability, for return loads east from San Antonio. Not only could surface transportation never have created that new business. It now hauls the farmer fertilizer he formerly did not need.

The integration of eastern manufacture with western flowers, fruits, and vegetables is only one facet of the new potential.

Few perishables are more sensitive than style itself. Today a San Francisco merchant can place advertising for day after tomorrow's sale of dresses that are still in New York. They will be on his racks when the store opens. Thanks to the containers developed by air freighters, they will not require pressing before sale.

Much conventional boxing and crating is obviated in air freight. The savings often exceed the difference between air tariff and the Less Than Carload Lot classification which is unprofitable to most surface transportation. For a detailed answer to the question "What is air cargo?" the reader might thumb the catalogues of the large mail-order houses. Even at the 20- to 10-cent rate, they now use air freight extensively. A categorical answer is simpler; air cargo is new wealth. . . .

Commercial aviation began with a necessary load of subsidy upon the shoulders of every taxpayer. Air freight can be made to carry that load. The wings that do it will be lifting both the strength and the prestige of free enterprise, to the profit of the free world.

By doing that we should find the vision to make air freight, through mutually profitable distribution of the resources over which men fight, carry its ultimate load of peace.

HURRY UP AND SAVE [7]

In . . . [1957] the long-awaited boom in air cargo was getting off the ground.

The palmy days of the first postwar years (when probably one thousand carriers were in the air) had faded. But the handful of all-freight lines left were either making money or reaching for the black ink, and big trunk carriers like American Airlines— No. 1 freight and passenger hauler—confidently expected this

[7] From "Nobody Wants to Wait," article by John A. Conway, associate editor of *Newsweek*. *Newsweek*. 50:86-7. October 21, 1957. Reprinted by permission.

year's cargo traffic to soar 30 to 35 per cent over 1956. The planemakers, who up to now have concentrated on the human angle—today's flying boxcars are basically modified passenger planes—now are hard at work peddling designs engineered specifically for the box-and-barrel trade.

"Speed" and "emergency" still rank at the top of the air shipper's lexicon. "Nobody want to wait for anything these days," says Miami's John Paul Riddle, whose Riddle Airlines . . . [expected] to top $60 million in 1957. But the emergency that sets off today's rush shipment is part of the United States industrial routine, where meticulous, split-second programming is the rule. Two weeks ago, president John C. Emery of Emery Air Freight reports, he had to rush 25,000 pounds of automobile doors to California—and wasn't surprised. "In auto production," he explains, "emergencies are created by the nature of the business. Air freight solves the emergencies." R. M. Stevens, a Ford traffic man, backs him up: "The more people and plants you acquire, the more air shipments will be required. Human error alone, as slight as it may be, assures that."

The nation's air freighters have found that the balance sheet, and not the wild blue yonder, makes the most effective selling pitch. "Everybody has been cutting manufacturing costs," says American Airlines vice president Samuel C. Dunlap, "but they haven't done nearly as much in distribution." Flying Tiger president Robert W. Prescott, a veteran of Major General Claire Chennault's China fighters, would agree. "Our first customers," Prescott says, "were the traffic managers, but more and more we're finding the company treasurer comes to us. He is the one who learns how to save money for his company, and who knows in a time of tight money how important shorter pipelines of stocks are."

To make their point, the airlines cite cases like Cleveland's Curtis Industries, Inc., a key maker and auto-accessory firm that closed down its warehouse in California in favor of air freight—and found it saved almost $120 a ton on West Coast shipments, another $150 a week on clerical costs of handling back orders under the old system. Gibson Art Company, the Cincinnati greeting-card manufacturer, found it could match deliveries of a competitor—without paying to match the rival's West Coast warehousing. By taking to the air, Spirella Corporation, a Niagara Falls corset maker, added $20,000 to gross profit—and less than $6,000 to costs. From its Atlanta warehouse, Sears, Roebuck uses Teletype and Riddle's air freighters to give overnight service to twenty-eight of its Florida outlets, a system that, according to Sears' Atlanta supervisor Bill Workman, usually jumps sales 30 per cent when introduced. "We find local stores can stock high-volume items in depth in the space usually required by products with less turnover. And we can bring in fringe products by air" (e.g., farm tractors, burros).

On the ocean runs, the air freighter can pay off even more handsomely. Eleven years ago, brothers Raymond and Arthur Norden pooled $20,000 and their wartime Air Transport Command experience to form Seaboard & Western, the only scheduled all-freight carrier on the North Atlantic (Pan Am, KLM, Sabena, Swissair, and TWA fly both cargo and passenger planes). Last year, the Nordens grossed $18.7 million, and in the first half of 1957 boosted operating earnings 59 per cent with revenues of $12 million (net: $662,000). More important, freight will bulk larger and larger, the cargo men think. (Even the all-freight lines have been making only about 40 per cent of their gross from cargo, the rest from charters, government contracts, used-plane sales, engine overhaul.)

This growth seems to be taking off from solid ground. In its short history—American filed the first United States air-freight tariff in 1944—the industry has changed from a helter-skelter, fire-horse operation into a genuine transportation system. (Actually, Air Express, a division of the Railway Express Agency, began shipping by 1927, and did a $42 million volume last year. But this flood of packages is classed separately from freight in airline operations.) The bulk of Seaboard's first business, Arthur Norden recalls, was in such items as Paris fashions. Today, this is still big—but instead of 90 per cent, it accounts for little more than half the traffic. The rest is hard goods—machinery, spare parts, Belgian glass for United States television tubes, radio resistors from Germany. New York dress manufacturers, Norden says, have worked out a whole new scheme of operation with air

With one-fourth more aircraft than all domestic commercial airlines combined, the military airline operates scheduled and nonscheduled passenger and cargo flights throughout the United States and 37 other nations along 110,000 miles of air routes. . . .

Besides its passengers and cargo transport service, the Command operates a variety of other services including weather reconnaissance, air rescue, photography and charting, aircraft ferrying, flight testing new equipment, and so-called special mission flights. The Command was created on July 1, 1948. To it was delegated the responsibility of providing all branches of the armed forces and other agencies of the United States Government with effective air transportation. It has world headquarters at Andrews Air Force Base in Maryland, just outside Washington, D.C.

The Hoover Commission said that most of the government airline routes were parallel to those of United States commercial air carriers.

The Hoover investigation found, for example, that an Air Force band was flown once a month from Westover, Massachusetts, to Bermuda. There was no band in Bermuda and the flights were justified by the Air Force for morale purposes.

The Commission did not challenge the justification but noted that two United States airlines which operate regular schedules along the route could have transported the band at less cost to the taxpayers.

The Hoover task force on air transportation learned further that commercial airline payments amounting to $42.9 million in fiscal 1954 could have been reduced 88 per cent if the airlines had flown only 25 per cent of the passenger volume and 50 per cent of the mail moved by MATS in the course of the year.

Today the government-operated airline provides service to Asia, Europe, Alaska, Africa, South America, the United Kingdom, and the Pacific Ocean area.

Assets of the government airline now total $1,468,280,529.

This includes $990,420,529 for aircraft and $477,860,000 for stocks, land, construction in progress, and other property. The figure is described as including certain property of other

Air Force units stationed on MATS bases, but not including equipment stationed at bases of other Air Force units.

From 1954's cost of $481,400,000, annual operating expenditures increased to $560,024,000 for fiscal 1955. . . . Expenditures [for 1957] will total about $740 million.

Some estimates, however, place the total cost to taxpayers as high as $1 billion a year.

The gross operating expenditure is described as including costs for interceptor defense, air rescue, weather reconnaissance, air evacuation, aerial surveys, ferrying aircraft, and turboprop tests, in addition to transportation services. The operating figures do not include cost of depreciation on capital assets. Nor do they include salaries.

The Military Air Transport Service operates approximately 1,500 airplanes. All United States domestic commercial airlines combined operate 1,212.

Of the service's total, 506 are four-engine aircraft. All United States airlines together operate 548 four-engine planes.

The Navy operates 50 of the newer four-engine transports in regular passenger service. These are assigned to MATS. The Navy also has 149 of the C-54 type aircraft used during World War II. Another 36 twin-engine transports make up the Navy's air transport system. . . .

MATS has approximately 104,500 personnel assigned to it. These include Air Force and Navy personnel and civilian employees. In 1955 the service logged 1,180,000 hours flying time, a 24 per cent increase over 1954. Transport planes flew 568,000 hours, carrying 733,400 passengers and patients and moving 139,000 tons of cargo and mail. . . .

Like its commercial counterpart, the military schools flight attendants for duty on its planes. The flight attendant school at Palm Beach Air Force Base in Florida has trained more than 1,600 young men and women since the fall of 1952, when the training program was begun.

Service to the customer is stressed. The airwomen (WAF's) chosen for this duty are picked for their good appearance and winning personalities, two of the qualifications which the private airlines insist upon when selecting young women for stewardess training.

Two flight attendants are provided for each flight where passenger load is sixty-six or less. Regulations call for three qualified flight attendants on each aircraft where load exceeds sixty-six passengers.

In transporting military dependent personnel, rules say it is desirable that at least one flight attendant be a registered nurse.

Additional passenger conveniences are provided by carpeted floors (to insure comfortable floor-level temperatures), no less than one blanket and one pillow for each passenger, a supply of palliatives for relief of airsickness, clean headrests for each seat prior to loading, wash-room facilities, airsickness cups for each seat, and so on.

Meals are served in flight. Usually the passenger pays for each meal. The cost is 75 cents for all civilians and officers.

Enlisted personnel pay 40 cents per meal. Those, however, who are receiving no subsistence allowances are given meals at government expense. Meals for children cost 40 cents each.

Hot cakes with sausage, bacon or ham, eggs, cereal, beverages, and so on may be served for breakfast. Some planes feature pop-up toasters. Lunch may consist of soup or juice, beef or fowl, vegetables, salad, rolls, butter, beverage and dessert. Dinner features similar menus, except that regulations specify that the entree must be of a different variety than lunch.

Airplanes utilized for passenger operation are equipped with a galley suitable for preparation of such hot meals.

The Military Air Transport Service is organized into three divisions, the Atlantic, Pacific, and the Continental.

The Atlantic Division operates from the East Coast of the United States through Europe to the Middle East. It links up in Saudi Arabia with the Pacific Division, operating from the West Coast of the United States through Far East bases.

The Continental Division completes the network of global air routes. It operates from coast to coast and throughout the Western Hemisphere from Alaska to Rio de Janeiro, in Brazil. . . .

The activities of the Military Air Transport Service were brought out recently in hearings by a congressional subcommittee on Department of the Air Force appropriations. The committee noted in its report that "the controversial aspects of this service result primarily because, to some extent, it is competitive with commercial air facilities."

The committee recognized the strategic importance of the transport service.

At the same time [the committee noted] it is apparent that commercial air facilities, including scheduled and nonscheduled airlines, are an essential part of the over-all mobilization transport strength of the United States, and will provide a major part of the ability of the nation to meet the huge demands for transport in the event of a sudden war emergency.

Because of the significant role that the Military Air Transport Service plays in our mobilization planning, the committee does not desire to set an arbitrary limit on the size of the MATS operation.

However, it was the committee's opinion that the Air Force should handle its air transport business "in such a way as to assist in keeping the nonscheduled and other airlines in a reasonably sound financial and operating position."

MATS: TOO BIG AND TOO CHEAP [9]

Military Air Transport Service was formed in 1948 as a merger of the Air Transport Command and the Naval ATS, and embraced a number of weather, air rescue and ground operations of the Air Force, Army and Navy. Originally it was planned that MATS be a training organization, nucleus of a vast air fleet to supply logistical support—high-speed movement of men and materials to global battlefronts—in time of war or other national emergency.

This idea was endorsed with enthusiasm by Congress and the entire airline industry. Optimistic congressmen hoped that a centralized MATS would be a way to eliminate costly duplication of the armed services' efforts in the air transport field, and at the same time would materially improve what was then called the United States "defense posture."

At the same time, the United States air transport industry, growing by leaps and bounds as new routes were opened and

[9] From "MATS: Pentagon's Air Transport Monster," by Robert Burkhardt, transportation editor of *American Aviation*. *American Aviation*. 21:39-40. May 5, 1958. Reprinted by permission.

larger and faster planes came into service, saw in MATS a chance to work in partnership with the armed services. Out of this, it was hoped, might come a vigorous and healthy civilian air transport industry, backed by an existing system of overseas MATS bases—including weather reporting, air traffic control, air rescue service and other support functions—all operating in conjunction with a nucleus fleet of late-model MATS aircraft.

Not too much is known about early MATS equipment and schedules. . . . All told, 279 transports were taken over from Air Transport Command and the Naval ATS, mostly twin-engine Douglas-built C-47's and four-engine C-54's. Early schedules listed few and irregular flights.

This humble beginning was no drawback to MATS planners. Right from the start MATS set out to become the biggest airline in the world by the simple expedient of offering free rides and free freight. And the number of takers has increased by leaps and bounds; today MATS traffic includes the majority of all United States military personnel moving to and from stations overseas, plus officers of NATO and other allied forces, employees of the State Department and other government agencies, servicemen's wives and families, and everyone else who can qualify as a "guest of the government." Freight shipments and government mail follow the same pattern.

It wasn't intended this way. To make certain that MATS was in fact a military operation, geared for a manyfold expansion in time of war, a clear policy line was laid down by the Secretary of Defense, and reemphasized by the Secretary of the Air Force: as many military passengers and as much military freight as possible was to be shipped by regular commercial aircraft.

Service to out-of-the-way points, such as Thule and Ascension Island, was the job of MATS, since no commercial air line could take this traffic. And in time of peak loads, when the regular scheduled "common carriers by air" were jammed up and delays expected, MATS could fly the goods and carry the GI's.

Good idea, said Congress. Sound defense policy, said the commercial airlines. And they were right, except for one small detail: MATS has never paid any attention to these policies, although repeatedly reminded of them by responsible committees of Congress.

Thus it is no wonder that MATS has grown so fast it has today become larger than all United States overseas commercial air carriers put together. . . .

How have Congress and the airlines reacted to this? Repeatedly, Congress has tried to slow down the unchecked growth of MATS, only to be airily ignored. . . . As for the carriers, the reaction to MATS has been varied: a very few aroused and struggling; some quiet and inclined to ignore MATS insofar as possible; others in such terminal stages of financial ill health that they no longer care about MATS' dog-in-the-manger policies towards government passenger and freight traffic. . . .

Thoughtful airline spokesmen are quick to emphasize the fact that the growth of MATS need not be malignant. MATS is a key weapon in the United States anti-Soviet arsenal; perhaps it should be even bigger. Nobody—repeat, *nobody*—takes issue with the military job that is the primary responsibility of MATS.

But what is being viewed with increased fear by taxpayers, congressmen and airline officials alike, is the twisted concept now dominating the thinking of MATS' high command. This concept has now resulted in establishment of the largest state-owned airline in the world; one whose no-charge or nominal-charge policies are isolating and threatening to bankrupt its commercial competitors, and will continue to do so until either Congress or some other higher authority takes firm and corrective surgical action.

MOBILIZING FOR WAR [10]

Come an all-out war, the government has contracted to purchase an airlift package from the airline industry. The package is called CRAF, Civil Reserve Air Fleet.

[10] From "Aerial Lifeline in Reserve," by Brigadier General Milton W. Arnold (USAAF Ret.), vice president for operations and engineering of the Air Transport Association and wartime Chief of Operations of the Second Air Division, Eighth Air Force. *Air Force.* 39:17-21. June 1956. Reprinted with permission from *Air Force* Magazine, official journal of the Air Force Association, Mills Building, Washington 6, D.C.

CRAF is made up of a fleet of airliners capable of moving men, machines, and materiel to the four far corners in a civilian-operated airlift, the like of which the world has never known before. Operationally, it is a plan worked out jointly by the Department of Defense, the Department of Commerce, and the operators of our civilian air transportation system.

The plan calls for integrating commercial airliners and the know-how of the air transport industry into the Military Air Transport Service's aerial supply line whenever it is necessary to support an emergency action. At the same time, a war air service pattern for the remaining civil airliner fleet is being worked out, designed to insure essential priority air traffic over the 80,000 miles of domestic airline routes and the 112,000 miles of our international system.

In short, the CRAF plan calls for taking the experience, manpower, and facilities of the commercial airlines and using them to augment the military airlift capacity (MATS), which would be taxed in the early stages of another war.

In the words of Lieutenant General Joseph Smith, the Commander of MATS, who is charged with implementing the entire CRAF program, "CRAF is a mobilization of civil airlines *capability*. It is *not* a militarization of the airlines."

The plan provides for:

Orderly, yet rapid, transition of the civil airlines from normal schedules to contractual military support operations.

Limited modification of selected four-engine civil aircraft so that equipment for long-range, over-ocean operation could be installed quickly.

Assignment of actual routes and destinations to the civilian operators so that each airline can plan for the routes over which its aircraft will be flying.

Deferment for essential airline operating personnel, as much as possible, from active military service.

Already certain phases of the CRAF program are in motion. There are still many things to be worked out, but the basic formula is off the runway and heading in the right direction. If needed, CRAF could be put into operation this minute!

Many of its planes, for example, have been tagged by N-number for the job. More than 80 per cent of these planes have been modified to provide for a different kind of operation than their normal duties require. New planes have the necessary modifications built in, engineered, as a matter of fact, from their blueprint stages. The Lockheed Super G Constellations, for example, were designed with "quick conversion" interiors. In a matter of hours it could go from a sixty-five passenger capacity to more than one hundred.

CRAF planes aren't mothballed. It is not a stand-by operation. These planes are busy day and night flying mail, passengers, air express, and freight. They constitute more than 45 per cent of the civilian air industry's four-engined fleet. CRAF planes every day are flying routes which at any moment might become vital new war supply lines.

Likewise, ground personnel, flight crews, station facilities, and maintenance operations have been keyed to the CRAF plan. Rendezvous points, hopping-off points, loading points, maintenance bases, and other operational tasks have been assigned specific carriers. As rapidly as possible, needed equipment and materials for the operation of the reserve air fleet are being stockpiled. Although flight crews have not been classified by name, pilots, copilots, flight engineers, navigators, and all flight personnel have been "alerted" and know they might be called on overnight. . . .

To understand CRAF we have to go back to . . . the Civil Aeronautics Act of 1938. . . . The Act gave purpose and mission to the airlines under a system of regulated competition and rigid safety requirements. Its ultimate aim was, and is, that the industry will become self-sufficient while serving the commerce, the postal system, and the national defense of the United States. Congress spelled out definite obligations that the air transport industry must perform as a defense partner.

Before it was three years old—still in the kindergarten of regulated competition under the Civil Aeronautics Act—air transport went to war. Six months after Pearl Harbor, more than half our commercial fleet—193 planes out of 359—was either sold outright or leased to the government. One-third of the airline personnel, top executives, pilots, radio operators, flight superintendents, meteorologists, and maintenance crews went into uniform. Their know-how formed the nucleus of the Air Transport Command (ATC) and the Naval Air Transport Service (NATS), predecessors of today's world-wide MATS operations. Airline experience pioneered new air routes across the top of the world and around its hot, equatorial middle. It developed new techniques of flying, navigation, maintenance, at home and abroad, and helped write the bible for a global network of air transport.

By war's end, on Army and Navy errands, the airlines had flown the equivalent of 26,000 times around the world. They flew 8 billion passenger-miles and 850 million ton-miles of cargo. They moved anything and everything that would fit into a plane's fuselage. World War II was the proving ground for a whole new concept of logistics.

It proved, beyond any doubt, the value of an air transport industry in being and showed how it could be used in time of national emergency.

On the strength of this a number of government agencies and the airline industry itself began studying how to prepare the airlines for a future emergency.

The big concern was to eliminate the obvious mistakes of World War II. As somebody put it, "Then the airlines weren't drafted—they were atomized."

Too many planes were taken away from civilian war jobs too quickly. There was no world-wide route pattern in the beginning because there were only one or two over-ocean routes. Planes and crews got to places in a hurry, only to sit around and sweat out loading, maintenance, and uncalled-for operational delays. There was no system of air priorities worked out until months later. Airline know-how was scattered in a thousand directions before it could be collected to a single purpose.

In any future war, there would be no time to get organized. Needed air transport must be ready, on the shelf. This was proved in Korea. Using civil air transport for the Korean airlift was a sample of how ready-made and ready-for-action airlift could be used by contracting with the carriers.

This is the crux of the CRAF plan which came into being officially in 1951 after many discussions and surveys by the Department of Defense, Department of Commerce, and the civilian air transport industry. The result, CRAF, is a many-sided operation, organically. It is directed and supervised by the MATS Commander acting as an operating agency for the Department of Defense. Its operational control is under MATS. However, it is maintained and operated by the civilian air transport companies, using their personnel, planes, facilities, and experience on a contract basis. All activities are coordinated with a civilian agency, the Defense Air Transport Administration (DATA), acting for the Department of Commerce. Another agency to handle necessary air priorities is being established under jurisdiction of the CAB. . . .

The physical requirements of CRAF are continuously changing. Based on 1956 figures, however, the CRAF fleet will consist of more than 360 four-engined, overseas aircraft with a contingency reserve of 35 additional aircraft to replace losses. These include Douglas DC-4's and DC-6's, Lockheed Constellations, Boeing Stratocruisers, and the newer and larger DC-7's and Super Constellations.

Their airlift capacity has been estimated at 566,000 available ton-miles per hour. But the figure is being revised upwards to around 797,000 available ton-miles per hour on the basis of the proposed 1956-1957 CRAF program that will include more of the bigger and faster planes.

Revised estimates indicate the numerical size of the fleet may be increased to at least 358 planes, but its airlift capacity will go up 39 per cent while the number of planes increases by only 13 per cent. "We are trying to keep virtually the same number of coins in our emergency fund," a DATA spokesman explained, "but we're putting in quarters instead of dimes."

Jet transports will eventually again double the capacity without substantially increasing the number. And CRAF planners are already counting on using jets in the reserve fleet. . . .

Modification of the planes for CRAF has been in progress for more than three years, by the airlines under government contract at airline maintenance and overhaul bases. This program involves installation of necessary wiring and brackets so that the peacetime airliners can accept military equipment. Such equipment includes new electronic systems, navigational aids, and sea-rescue gear necessary for over-ocean operations.

Initial pre-D-Day modification—brackets and wiring—adds about fifty pounds extra weight to the airliner. But the equipment itself will weigh almost half a ton. The fact that the planes are equipped to accept the extra "black boxes," however, puts the reserve fleet that much closer to active readiness. It means planes unequipped to fly the ocean today can be fitted to fly anywhere in forty-eight hours.

CRAF is a two-ocean operation, with an Atlantic Division and a Pacific Division. The routes for each division have already been designated. In addition to normal airline routes, several auxiliary routes have been selected exclusively for CRAF use. The airliners responsible for operating their planes over all the respective routes have their assignments. Likewise various airlines have been assigned as Senior Lodgers for each division—responsible for upkeep of CRAF bases which will become maintenance and refueling stops and necessary equipment stockpile centers for the operation.

Sixteen different airlines have been assigned to the Atlantic Division and eight other companies have been assigned to the Pacific Division. Some operators provide services for both areas. Altogether, twenty-four different airlines participate in the CRAF program. The majority are scheduled airline operators with the remainder coming from the nonscheduled and contract haulers. Each has its specific assignment. . . .

Equipment and supplies are being stockpiled at the various bases around the globe. Likewise, stockpiling of the necessary equipment for modification of the planes at the airlines' major overhaul bases has also been in effect. Under the contract arrangement the government pays for this equipment, the stockpiling, the necessary modification work. But the civilian operators provide the planes and crews and put it to use. . . .

Personnel problems have recently been clarified to some extent. All airline pilots, other than those serving in a supervisory capacity, are definitely earmarked for duty with the CRAF program. No longer are personnel in this category "counted twice," i.e., they may no longer fill positions as mobilization designees within the Air Force structure while being counted as a CRAF crew member. Several plans are under consideration to further resolve the draft and reserve status of airline personnel other than air crew members.

Suffice it to say, everything possible is being done to keep essential personnel of the airlines for the CRAF operation in their jobs which can give maximum efficiency to the program. The whole theory of CRAF is based on the principle of utilizing experience and know-how to the highest degree.

The man who would actually trigger CRAF is the Commander of MATS. But he will not set the program into motion without an executive order passed on to him through the Department of Defense.

A full-scale war is the real test. Here's how CRAF would work for the first forty-eight hours:

(1) All CRAF planes, wherever they might be, would return to or head toward designated modification points (the respective airline maintenance centers) where necessary equipment for overseas operation would be installed.

(2) All CRAF crews would be alerted and flown to already designated flyaway points.

(3) Senior Lodgers at the various overseas bases would be alerted and ready to receive the flow of CRAF traffic.

(4) As soon as the modification program was completed on each aircraft it would be flown to designated rendezvous points or assigned to a specific mission.

Simultaneously the war air service pattern for the remaining civilian fleet would go into effect under a priorities system.

This is the plan. This is CRAF. It is being revised and revitalized every day. How well it will work can only be learned when and if we ever have to use it.

III. JETS AND BEYOND

EDITOR'S INTRODUCTION

"This is the apogee of flight," said a western newspaper in 1927. "A single engine and a single wing have carried man across the raging Atlantic and in twenty-four short years brought the Wright brothers' great invention to its ultimate refinement."

The event that inspired this clouded praise was Lindbergh's flight from New York to Paris, and *The Spirit of St. Louis* was scarcely in its hangar at Le Bourget before advances in aviation had made it obsolete. For aviation has no predefined limit. Man's conquest of the air has already passed the air itself and his horizon has soared from the next dune at Kitty Hawk to the next galaxy in space. No newspaper today would dare circumscribe the possibilities of flight and no true scientist ever has. All science can do and will do, basing its conclusion solely on an extension of what we already know, is to make an educated guess at what might happen in the foreseeable future.

In the section that follows, the "foreseeable future" of a decade ago is described in being and its portents evaluated. Only ten years ago the jet liner that Wolfgang Langewiesche describes in the opening article was hardly a dream and the problems it would engender—described by the editors of *Business Week* in "Spending Money to Make Money" and "But No Place to Land" —would have been an airline's nightmare. These problems, and these challenges, are already international in their scope—as the editors of *Fortune* explain in "Jets Across the Sea"—and the three concluding articles indicate that they will multiply almost in perpetuity. They will multiply because each new advance in aviation, such as the machines for vertical flight analyzed by Francis Bello in "The Shape of Things to Come," begets new problems and sets new goals. These goals, so far as the airlines of America are concerned, and as Richard Tregaskis points out in "The Next Fifty Years," will be limited by man's economic and physical capacity to attain them. So far as science is concerned there are no limits.

THE JET LINER [1]

You'll find the takeoff in a jet disappointing. No mighty force pulls you back into your seat, as on the propeller airplane. The acceleration is sluggish. And the run is so long you begin to take alarm. Is something wrong? Won't she fly?

It's all right. You've met the jet engine's main characteristic, and the reason why many cities are planning to build longer runways: the jet airplane has got to *be* going before it can really *get* going. The jet airplane behaves like a car with only one gear—high. It thrives on speed.

After the pilot lifts it off the ground at 165 miles per hour, the liner begins to show its stuff. It keeps speeding up—to 300 miles per hour—as it also climbs. The noise, loud on takeoff because it reverberated from the ground, has now faded out. In a few minutes all familiar landmarks are far behind and deep below. The airplane becomes a time-capsule.

Typical cruise is at 36,000 feet, 575 miles per hour. This is twice as high and almost twice as fast as the big propeller ships fly. The speed *sensation* is therefore the same—mild. But the results! New York-Paris, seven and a half hours. Paris-New York, a little slower because of winds, is even better because of the six-hour time difference. Leave after the theater; arrive New York in time for a night's sleep!

You look at such a machine with respect. Every line has a purpose. Why those swept-back wings? They work the way a safety razor does as it slides sidewise over the skin. It cuts better that way. The swept-back wing cuts through the air in that same sidewise-slicing fashion, and becomes in effect thinner, sharper and more knife-like.

This wing is an engineering marvel. It's hollow and is at the same time the airplane's fuel tank. It holds an incredible seventy tons of kerosene—as much as four big highway tank-trucks. It is also elastic. The airplane rides on it as if on springs; it cushions the effect of rough air which, on stiff wings at 550 miles per hour, could be a vicious slamming.

[1] From "Let's Ride the New Jet Liner," article by Wolfgang Langewiesche, instrument test pilot and author. *Reader's Digest.* 73:58-62. July 1958. Copyright 1958 by The Reader's Digest Association, Inc. Condensed from *Harper's Magazine.* 216:50-6. June 1958. Reprinted by permission.

The jet liner does not break the sound barrier. It stays just this side of it. Economical Cruise will be at 82 per cent of sound (speed), Fast Cruise at 88 per cent. How fast is that? Sound speed varies with air temperature. Under average conditions, at 36,000 feet, the two speeds will be 541 miles per hour and 581 miles per hour.

The jet liner has a new thing: *two* ailerons on each wing—two of those control surfaces that bank and unbank the airplane. One is in the usual position at the wing-tip; the other more inboard. Why two? For slow flight, the control surfaces should be big, or control is too sluggish. For fast flight ailerons should be small. The two at the wing-tips are for slow speed work, the inboard two for high speed. When the pilot puts the flaps down for landing, his control wheel automatically connects with the slow-speed ailerons.

But why jet engines in the first place? After all, the regular airplane engine was the most nearly perfect mechanism ever made. One answer: The conventional piston engine hit a power ceiling during World War II—at about 4,000 horsepower. Most successful engines are below that. This is because a piston engine can achieve such power only by an unbelievably complex piling of parts upon parts. The jet engine packs three or four times as much power as the piston engine, and does so in a smaller, lighter package. This more powerful engine makes it possible to build a bigger plane, and the liner's size is as important as its speed in making it economic.

Another answer: Propeller-driven planes have a speed limit of about 450 miles per hour because the propeller blade—which goes faster than the airplane—hits the sound barrier, and its efficiency rapidly fades out.

The propeller airplane drives itself forward by pushing air backward. So does the jet. But instead of using heat to move mechanical devices which move surfaces which finally shove air— the jet shoves the air *by heat direct*. It simply takes in air at its front end, mixes it with fuel and sets it on fire; and the exploding mixture puffs out the back end. It is a marvelous short cut. . . .

How safe is a jet? To be licensed as an airliner, an airplane has to comply with a thick book of safety regulations, very detailed, very exacting. As far as safety is measurable beforehand, then, a jet liner is as safe as any plane flying today.

But everyone remembers the early Constellation and DC-6 troubles, the Comet disasters. In newly designed, radically different airplanes, bugs often show up in actual service. They are not necessarily dangerous ones. And some planes have slid into service with almost none. An example is the Vickers Viscount, at the time of its introduction a radically new airplane.

One thing is certain: as the new wears off, the gains remain. In the case of jet liners, the gains are particularly impressive. What are they?

Number one: no more propeller. The propeller has become complicated and the most dangerous part of the airplane. Here is the problem: in pulling the airplane, it also performs the services of a gearshift. On takeoff, it works in low, in the cruise, in overdrive. If an engine fails, it goes into neutral. During the landing run, the propellers can be put in reverse and used as a brake. While it works, it's very good; but if it doesn't work, it's horrid!

When engines fail and propellers do *not* "feather" (go into neutral), the airplane is difficult to control and may be unable to hold altitude. Worse, engines have *not* failed and the propeller *did* "feather." Propellers have gone into reverse during the approach glide; have also come apart in the air. They have suddenly gone into low in cruising flight; the braking effect then is terrific, and if it happens over the ocean, the airplane may be unable to reach land. In a jet, with no propeller, all these possibilities are gone.

Gain number two: a more reliable engine. Jet engine troubles usually show up many hours beforehand as small discrepancies in the instrument readings. So engine troubles can be caught early, and engine failure in flight—rare anyway—will practically never happen.

Gain number three: more speed, more altitude. Weather forecasts to the pilot are more reliable because they are made less far ahead. Altitude, too, is an element of mastery. For twenty-five years, airlines have dreamed of "over-weather flight." The jets, flying at 35,000 feet, will practically make it. They still can't top *all* weather. Some thunderstorms reach 60,000 feet. But, up there, they appear as isolated cloud-towers, easy to go around. The jets will cruise in sunshine practically all the time.

The early Comet was a victim of high altitude and the pressurized air inside its cabin. A hairline crack opened up in a window frame, and as the result of the air pressure instantly grew into a rip many feet long that tore the whole airplane wide open. It exploded.

All concerned have thoroughly learned their lesson. The new jet liners have metal skins 70 per cent thicker than the first Comet had. And, if there *is* a leak, they have a second line of defense—called rip-stopping. Suppose you tear up an old shirt: once started the tear grows easily until you come to a seam. Translated from fabric to metal, that's "rip-stopping." The skin is criss-crossed (on the inside of the fuselage) by a network of metal strips, one every ten inches or so. Each strip acts like that seam. If a crack starts, it can grow but only to the nearest strip, not across it. It just makes a hole; it doesn't rip the airplane apart.

The jet's brakes are marvels: if braking makes the wheels skid, the brake feels that, lets go for a moment, and grabs hold again the instant the skid has stopped. Too, the jet liner has "thrust reversers" to take the job of the reversible propeller. Behind each engine, folded away during flight, rides a clam-shell shaped scoop. After landing, this drops into place, catches the jet blast and bends it around forward, thereby holding the airplane back.

SPENDING MONEY TO MAKE MONEY [2]

On June 7, 1955, a directors' meeting of Douglas Aircraft Company instructed Donald Douglas to go ahead and build America's first passenger jet. And just over a month later, the United States Air Force told Boeing Airplane Company it had no objection to Boeing's building commercial jets concurrent with military production.

[2] From "With the Whoosh of the Jets the Airlines Grow Up." *Business Week.* p 156-70. July 21, 1956. Reprinted by permission of *Business Week,* a McGraw-Hill publication. Copyright 1956 by McGraw-Hill Publishing Company.

Today, with a speed that has surprised even the experts, these large fast passenger planes are definitely and inescapably on the way. . . .

Airlines have committed over $1.5 billion for these planes, plus spare parts. They'll have to invest millions more in accessory equipment, training, maintenance bases, and merchandising before they can begin to fly them and reap profits from them.

Expenses won't end there. Taxpayers and investors will be called upon for additional billions to finance new and bigger airport facilities. The airfields themselves will have to be enlarged. Even today, during peak periods at a few of the nation's busiest airports, there isn't room on the ground for all the planes wanting to take on or discharge passengers. Terminal facilities are already badly overcrowded. When the jets come in they'll be carrying bigger loads than the largest of today's commercial airliners. Confusion and delays in the passenger terminals will get much worse unless they, too, are enlarged. . . .

Almost since the beginning of passenger flying, aviation's rate of growth and the load it puts on ground facilities have consistently been underestimated. The jets now on order are so large and so fast that if facilities to handle them aren't improved and enlarged, chaos may well result. Some think chaos is inevitable.

The Jet's Big Goal—Economy

Why are airlines buying these costly and radically different planes, when with them they're getting operational and financial headaches? The answer is that the advantages of the jets are so great and that commercial aviation is so competitive that the big well-entrenched airlines can afford to buy them, and the smaller trunklines can't afford not to. . . .

Greater Speed. The Boeing and Douglas jets are capable of cruising between 550 miles per hour and 600 miles per hour. That's 200 miles per hour to 250 miles per hour faster than today's piston engine transports. The smaller Convair jet reportedly will fly at 607 miles per hour.

The jet's higher speed will increase each plane's revenue. Because each jet flies faster it should be able to fly more frequently. While one of today's planes is making two Atlantic crossings, for example, a jet could make three.

But this is just one way of increasing revenue with jets. A jet will cut almost in half the time it takes to fly across the United States. Airline executives are convinced that vacationers and businessmen who might not make the trip today can be expected to make it in 1961. Certainly many people who wouldn't have flown across the United States five years ago are making the transcontinental air trip now.

Douglas has even suggested to airlines that weekends in Paris will be a selling point when the Douglas DC-8 is flying. The attraction, says Douglas, is that a flight leaving New York at 8 P.M. Friday night would arrive at Paris early Saturday morning; would leave Paris at 10 P.M. on Sunday and, because of the time differential, would land in New York at 11:30 the same night.

As travel becomes easier, then, airline executives are confident more people will travel.

Greater Range. Manufacturers claim the larger, intercontinental versions of their two planes will be able to fly with a full payload and normal fuel reserves more than 4,000 miles. By comparison, today's Douglas DC-6B has a range of about 3,500 miles.

Eventually, when and if international airlines are equipped entirely with long-range jet airliners, costly mid-flight fueling bases can be closed.

However, the first of the jet airliners will not have so great a range as the piston-engine aircraft now being introduced to commercial runs. Douglas' DC-7C, the first of which went into transatlantic service . . . [in 1956] for Pan American World Airways, has a range of 4,800 miles. And Lockheed Aircraft Corporation has a super Super-Constellation, designated 1649A, capable of flying 6,300 miles. The reason the first of the jet series won't match the range of what is probably the last of the piston-engine series is that the jets burn fuel in prodigious amounts, especially at low altitudes.

Greater Capacity. The biggest of present four-motor planes can seat up to 90 or so tourist passengers. Boeing advertises that its overseas jet, the Intercontinental 707, will seat at least 146 passengers in tourist configuration and, by squeezing, airlines can probably fit more.

The true importance of this can be seen by a pair of facts issued by the International Civil Aviation Organization.

A single large jet will have approximately the same annual transatlantic passenger-carrying capacity as a 40,000-ton ocean liner such as the *Ile de France*.

Twelve of these aircraft, it is estimated, could handle all today's air traffic over the North Atlantic. . . .

And a Great Upheaval. For all the advantages that airlines expect to get from the jets, they'll create an upheaval, a predictable chaos, when they begin flying.

These periods of upheaval due to lack of preparation in one field for swift advances in another aren't exactly unfamiliar in United States economic history. For decades there has been the example of the auto industry and the highways. Detroit has kept turning out cars by the millions every year; at no time has the highway system been capable of carrying all these cars without traffic jams, confusion, and much accidental bloodshed.

The upheaval that's bound to come with the advent of the jets needn't run wild. The United States has two or three years to prepare for the jets' entry into regular commercial flying. The airlines are hoping that the airports, the control systems, the terminals, and the whole method of getting passengers and their baggage into and out of airliners can be prepared so they will at least begin to cope with the jets' demands. Since the airlines are putting billions of dollars into the new planes, they're determined to do all they can to see that their investment isn't wasted through lack of preparation on the ground.

Paying the Bills

Already, well before the jets are in large-scale production, the airline executives have worked out a major change in their method of doing business—to take care of just one of the demands that the jets make.

This change has come in the airlines' financing methods, and it has been forced on them by the fact that these radically new airplanes carry radically high price tags.

The Douglas DC-3, which, more than any other airplane, put airlines in the passenger-hauling business, cost about $125,000 when new. It flew 180 miles per hour, had a range of five hundred miles, and carried seats for twenty-one pasengers. As Douglas stretched out its DC series, it was also obliged to raise the price tag. The postwar DC-4, seating forty-four passengers, cost $475,000. . . . The DC-6 went for $860,000 and the DC-6B went over the million mark with a $1,175,000 tag. . . . The first DC-7 cost about $1,850,000, while the DC-7C has raised the price of big piston-engine planes to $2,233,000. The jet, however, leaves even the highest of these figures far behind. The DC-8's and Boeing 707's now on order will cost from $5 million to $6 million each, with spare parts. The question is how to pay for this equipment.

In the past, equipment was paid for out of reinvested earnings, cash accumulations from fast depreciation and tax amortization certificates, equity financing, and short-term bank credits. Even the latter were liquidated rapidly out of earnings. Only infrequently were these methods supplemented by long-term debt, and then the maximum term was twenty years.

By these methods most airlines have been able to keep up in the equipment race.

Time for a Change. But these methods won't do any more. The jets, the necessary facilities to handle them, plus nonrecurring items such as pilot training, will be too costly, too steep a jump to handle by old financial policies.

Even selling many of today's piston-engine airplanes won't provide the funds the airlines need for the capital expansion that jets demand.

The airlines have had to borrow long before they're able to start flying the jets they've ordered because airplane manufacturers must get progress payments from the airlines.

This forces airlines to borrow heavily against future earnings. More important, management must commit millions of borrowed dollars to buy planes whose earnings can still be figured only from slide rule computations, not from flying experience. When most of the orders were placed, Boeing, Douglas, and Convair were still very much in the design stages of their jet aircraft.

If airlines had gone to banks and insurance companies a few years ago and asked to borrow for an equipment purchasing plan of this nature, money would not have been so readily available.

Today, however, this situation is changed. The major lines with the biggest jet buying plans have had little difficulty in arranging big loans for terms up to forty years at rates comparable to older, less volatile industries.

It has been easy because airlines have convinced the big lenders that theirs is going to be the mass medium of transportation. Jets for long hauls and some medium hauls, turboprops for short and medium runs, steeply-rising and vertically-rising aircraft and helicopters for interurban and commutation service—all these are either in use today or just over the horizon.

Travel by air is due to become so quick and easy, everyone will fly. That means commercial trunk airlines, or the ones that survive the inevitable growing pains, should become huge companies. That, in turn, means they need and can support long-term debt. . . .

Smaller domestic trunks and foreign airlines aren't being left out in the cold, either. Many banks, insurance companies, and investment bankers have either lent money or expressed willingness to do so.

Though the jets are expected to earn more per passenger-mile than today's planes, these increased earnings won't begin until at least 1959. Meanwhile, airline management must continue paying off its present-day equipment besides paying for the jets. And later, when the jets are flying, fast depreciation won't be possible. Most airlines today write off their planes in five to seven years. Expectations are that jets will have to be depreciated over at least ten years.

Pinch for Stockholders. All this means that financing needs have soared. And just as stockholders—having "starved" for years as airlines raced to keep up with the latest in planes—were ready to sit down to a banquet, the dining room doors have been slammed in their faces.

Whether the airlines can meet the terms of the loans they have negotiated for their jet transports depends on . . . whether airports can be enlarged fast enough to handle the heavier loads and more frequent trips of the new planes, on whether air traffic can be improved fast enough for them to get full service out of the jets, and on whether there'll be sufficient passengers to fill the big new planes.

But now that the big lenders of the United States have underwritten them, the larger airlines are hardly likely to be put out of business for failing to meet the terms of their loans for a year or two while their managements search for solutions to the major problems raised by the big changes that are coming in the air transportation business. Some smaller airlines might be badly hurt; some might even be forced into bankruptcy. The industry as a whole, many observers say, can't suffer.

Even the smaller airlines may survive. This depends first on the speed with which new airport facilities are built.

Getting Airborne

Airline managements and stockholders are less directly concerned in the financing of new and expanded airports than are local governments.

Most airports are too small already. In the jet age, they'll be hopelessly inadequate. They're too small now—and almost always have been—because aviation's rate of growth and the load it puts on ground facilities have consistently been underestimated. You don't have to look too far back to find some striking examples of this.

The Port of New York Authority, responsible for operating the city's four airports, forecast in 1950 that by 1955 domestic airlines would be flying a total of about 11 billion passenger-miles; and by 1965, some 16.7 billion passenger-miles. But by 1955, the actual figure for domestic trunk airlines was 19.9 billion passenger-miles.

More recently, St. Louis this spring completed a shiny, new, expandable terminal. At the opening ceremonies came this statement: "The building was designed to handle traffic volumes until 1960. Preliminary steps have already been taken to expand the structure because present indications are that traffic will reach that amount . . . this year."

Outgrown airports—notably Midway at Chicago, La Guardia at New York, and National at Washington, D.C.—irritate the customers and hit the airlines in the pocketbook. Delays in landing and taking off, out-dated loading and fueling procedures, and even the simple shortage of ramp space cut into maximum use of airplanes. When the bigger, faster, more expensive jets are in service it will be imperative that nonproductive ground time be cut to a minimum. . . . One group working on this problem sees a solution in trying to bypass airport terminals as much as possible. Jets burn so much fuel even in taxiing that it may prove more economical to leave them at "servicing stations" near the ends of runways. Passengers could be driven in buses direct to planeside from downtown locations.

Instead of fueling planes from gasoline trucks, which add to ground confusion at airports, jets would roll up to hydrants connected to large underground storage tanks.

A frequently more important consideration with today's too-small airports is runway length. . . . Though runways may not have to be lengthened everywhere, the increased size and speed of the commercial airlines' new planes, plus the yearly growth of airline traffic, still mean that most airports must be expanded. And that means that the public pocketbook must be tapped.

Jet's Voice. Generally, city airports are controlled by quasi-political bodies, sensitive to public opinion. If these authorities are to sell bonds for airport improvement, and if the Federal Government is to match these funds with taxpayers' money, the communities near the airports must at least accept, if not welcome, the jet age.

It's certain that communities won't accept living in close proximity to the new planes unless something is done about the jet engine's roar.

Cutting down the jet's voice is a management problem for airlines and manufacturers alike. It was spelled out years ago by Donald Lowe, chairman of the Port of New York Authority. He told airlines that jets would be refused permission to land at New York's airports unless they were quieted. . . . When Pan American World Airways signed the first contract for American-made jets, Lowe said: "It would be just as useless to design planes that cannot be operated into and out of metropolitan airports because of excessive noise or performance characteristics as it would be to design planes that cannot fly." . . .

Assuming the noise problem is licked and the public will be willing to pay to expand airports, airfields must be modernized to handle the increased number of planes and passengers efficiently. Most fields, barely caught up with the piston-engine plane, will have serious traffic problems—pedestrian, vehicular, and airborne—if they don't gear themselves to the jet.

Nobody knows what all the solutions are going to be—they don't even know yet what all the problems will be. But airlines and airports are working together to discover the problems and find the answers to them. . . .

Whether the jets will perform the way manufacturers have promised; whether all airlines will be able to finance the jets; [and] whether ground facilities will be ready for them . . . are all problems of the first rank.

Still, aviation men are confident they will be solved—though not without a struggle and some rough spots. The aviation industry is too young, too aggressive, and too used to problems to be stopped by such an upheaval as that caused by the jet age.

Finding the Passengers

But there's another problem, basic to the whole jet airline business, that has airline managements doing some deep soul-searching. The problem is: Will there be enough passengers to fill all the jets that the airlines have ordered?

To some observers, it seems that some airlines have ordered too many jets. These airlines, they say, have projected an average yearly increase in passenger-miles for the industry as a whole, then added another 5 per cent or 10 per cent to cover the increase they're expecting in their own business. This way, it is possible that the traffic projections of each airline, when added together, are considerably greater than what the industry thinks its total traffic will be by 1961.

This is particularly true for domestic airlines. In the past year competition has suddenly increased on domestic routes. The Civil

Aeronautics Board in case after case has opened or widened the door to competition where none or little existed before. United Air Lines has for years been the only transcontinental airline serving Denver, and Trans World Airlines has had a similar monopoly in Kansas City. Now TWA calls at Denver and United calls at Kansas City. This pattern is duplicated in dozens of other cities.

The question arises: What will these decisions do to each carrier's traffic predictions? No airline will willingly give up a single passenger to a new competitor. But any airline newly certificated to fly a route will be out to grab as much business as possible.

It's this prospect that has sent airline executives from big and little trunklines into the market place for jets.

If one line flying between two cities offers 550-mile-per-hour to 600-mile-per-hour service while another has 350-mile-per-hour equipment for the same ticket price, it's not hard to imagine what will happen to the slower line.

That is why smaller airlines seem, to some observers, to be faced with being swallowed up if they don't buy jets—and with possible bankruptcy if they do.

Predictions. It does not follow, however, that all airlines have bought too many jets. The heart of the question lies in finding the truth from the rash of forecasts of airline traffic that have been produced lately.

The CAA's official forecast of air traffic in 1961 is 28.8 billion passenger-miles. This is the most conservative estimate of all, and it represents only a 6 per cent average annual increase during the next five years.

But in the past five years, United States domestic trunk airlines have, on the average, increased their passenger mileage by 20 per cent a year. More important from the financial viewpoint, they have maintained a steady load factor—passenger-miles divided by seat-miles—the indicator of an airline's success in attracting passengers.

On this basis, the airlines have a rosier view of their future than the CAA. Indeed, the CAA is already questioning the accuracy of its forecast and plans to revise its estimate upward.

Middle Group. American Airlines' President C. R. Smith stands the middle ground on the question of what's ahead for the airlines. He says that by 1961, domestic trunklines will be flying 34.5 billion passenger-miles. That represents an average annual rate of growth of slightly less than 10 per cent for the next five years. And Smith says that if the customers are to get the best service, the domestic airlines will need to fly 55 billion seat-miles in 1961, at a load factor of almost 63 per cent.

One critic says, though, that when the jets are flying in 1961, the airlines will have a fleet capable of flying 75 billion seat-miles. This estimate includes the 30 billion seat-miles that airlines flew in 1955, plus the 45 billion seat-miles capacity of airplanes now on order.

American and most other carriers have a ready answer for this objection. They expect gradually to pull present-day airplanes from service.

Optimists. There are others in the industry who believe that Smith is being too conservative. [In August 1958 Mr. Smith gave evidence that he agreed: he signed contracts for fifty more medium-range jet planes for delivery by 1962—twenty-five from Convair, twenty-five from Boeing. He also introduced something new in plane financing: instead of buying the jet engines he will lease them from the engine manufacturer, saving American Airlines $80 million in capital outlay.—Ed.] Champion of the optimists is Captain Eddie Rickenbacker, board chairman of Eastern Air Lines.

Rickenbacker summed up his thinking not long ago:

In my opinion, the trend is now firmly fixed if we can provide the aircraft and the volume service needed to capitalize and profit from the tremendous potential demand for air transportation.

This is how he backs his opinion:

Only 8 million individuals accounted for the 35 million passengers that United States airlines flew in 1954. The bulk of these 8 million used the airlines for from two to twenty trips during the year. So in the 165 million population, there's a great number of potential new airline customers.

The new generations have been "born in the lap of aviation." The airplane is their most natural and preferred means of travel.

The United States population will reach 200 million by 1965, adding 35 million potential customers for everything the country produces, including air transportation, within the next ten years.

All this prompts Rickenbacker's forecast that:

Through the use of jet power and other technical improvements now within reach, air transportation should make more progress in the next ten years than we have been able to accomplish in the past twenty-five years. Within a year after the introduction of jet-powered air travel across the nation, the airlines will supersede surface transportation systems as the country's primary carrier of passengers.

Selling the Air

If Rickenbacker is right, and he has been so frequently in the past, the airlines have not ordered too many jets. But whoever is right about how big the market will be in 1961, one thing is certain. Airlines are going to have to merchandise their service in a way and to a degree they never have before.

To fill its planes each carrier must provide the optimum in service because that's all it has to sell when so many lines flying competing routes fly identical equipment and charge the same price.

To capture a bigger share of the travel market, airlines are going to have to speed up their reservations procedures, or, in the case of heavily traveled commuter runs, dispense with reservations altogether. They will have to speed up baggage handling and getting customers to and from airports. Finally, on an industry-wide basis to lure more travelers to the air, they will have to reduce fares.

With all these avenues open to them, and with the growth curve of their traffic rising so fast, it's plain that even if the airlines don't manage by 1961 to drum up all the traffic needed to fill their planes, they'll almost certainly get sufficient passengers by 1962 or 1963.

C. E. Woolman, one-time organizer of a crop dusting operation and now president of its successor, fifth-ranking Delta Air Lines said [in 1955]:

> We are buying airplanes that haven't been fully designed, with millions of dollars we don't have, and we are going to operate them off airports that are too small, in an air traffic control system that is too slow, and we must fill them with more passengers than we have ever carried before.

A few weeks later, Woolman purchased six DC-8's for Delta, later added two more to his order. And with that, Woolman neatly signified how the airlines feel today, one year after the jet age really began.

The jets are coming. And in their rush they'll mature the airlines faster than anything else ever could. Licking all the problems they'll bring will be one of the toughest jobs any group of managements has ever faced. The industry says it will do the job. Undoubtedly it will—because it has to.

BUT NO PLACE TO LAND [3]

"Did you hear about the new jet plane that will fly 12,500 miles per hour?" the first man asks. "It will take you to any point on earth in three hours."

"How come?" says the second man. "Halfway around the world is only 12,500 miles—that should be one hour."

"Yes"—and here comes the punch line—"but you spend one hour getting aboard the plane and another hour getting your bags at the other end."

Airlines don't like this kind of joke, especially on the eve of the new 600-mile-per-hour jet planes that will sharpen the contrast between speed in the air and stagnation on the ground. But the jokes will persist until ground travel to and from airports is speeded and the handling of passengers and baggage is greatly improved.

The carriers can't do much about the first problem, but passengers and baggage are their responsibility. The jet planes,

[3] From "Dream of Jet Age Airports Still Far from Reality." *Business Week.* p90-2+. November 30, 1957. Reprinted by permission of *Business Week,* a McGraw-Hill publication. Copyright 1957 by McGraw-Hill Publishing Company.

carrying twice as many passengers per trip, will make the problem just that much worse. And they also bring new problems that could revolutionize the airports. . . . By the end of 1959, United States lines are scheduled to be flying 78 jets; by 1961, the 287 jets now on order will all have been delivered to the airlines.

These jets are big. The Boeing 707's and Douglas DC-8's will carry from 109 to 178 passengers, depending on seating arrangements. The slightly smaller Convair 880's will carry 89 to 109 passengers and the newly announced Boeing 720's, 100 to 125 passengers. In comparison, the piston-engined DC-7 carries from 60 to 85 passengers. . . .

Much more than the airliners of today, the jets will be costly to keep on the ground. They are naturally noisy in taxiing and takeoffs, and it will cost money to muffle them. They burn upward of 2,000 gallons an hour, or three times as much as a DC-7 while in the air, and a substantial percentage of that while taxiing or waiting for takeoff. That's a consideration, too, when they have to be stacked over crowded airports.

Still, airlines have decided, they aren't going to be forced to operate from outlying airports because of their noise, nor will they have to be shut down while on the ground and the passengers ferried to and from them because the planes will be too expensive to taxi. Airlines say the jets won't even need special air traffic priorities because of their high fuel-consumption rate.

While the eight airlines with jets on order indicate that they expect to handle their jets much as they handle today's DC-7's and Super Constellations, their landlords—the airport operators—aren't so placid about the nature of the jet age.

The airport managers hear talk about a threefold increase in number of air travelers . . . [by] 1970. They hear complaints about present service, and they see a danger that ground accommodations will get worse before they get better. But they don't hear much from the people they think should be most concerned —their tenants, the airlines.

Unless the airlines make up their minds pretty soon about what they want and tell the terminal operators, the bright new day for the air traveler may be darkly clouded at dawn, says the Airport Operators Council.

Take runways, as a good example. It costs around $1,000 a running foot to lengthen a runway, and some airports may need to acquire more land to do so. Besides, it takes time even to build an extension on land already owned. Until the airport managers know for sure how much, if any, of this work will be necessary, they'll drag their feet on extending runways.

Need for length in runways depends on how heavy the jet liners will be at takeoff, and that in turn depends on how far the planes are going and how much reserve fuel they carry. So the airports really need to know what routes the airlines expect to fly from their runways.

Runways at present airports will be long enough in most cases, experts say, if the jets fly present routes and save 25 per cent of their fuel consumption by operating at the most economical speed, rather than the fastest. But if they are to develop their full potential of speed and range, the basic length of runway— 6,300 feet today—will have to stretch to around 7,700 feet. But . . . the airlines have so far been quite uncommunicative, if not abrupt, when queried by airport managers on their runway needs.

Most airports are owned by states, counties, or cities, sometimes through the medium of public authorities. It takes time for them to make plans, secure the all-important financing, and then construct the additional runway footage and build the other needed terminal improvements. Even New York's Idlewild International Airport, whose new units are just beginning to come into use, may not fully meet jet-age standards when its remodeling job is completed in 1959 or 1960.

Hushing the Jets

Forget the jets' thirst for fuel and their need for longer runways, and you still have to worry about a couple of items of airport housekeeping—some ways of quieting their engine blast so the neighbors and the customers can stand it, and some way of keeping the runways and ramps spotlessly free from debris that the air intakes could suck up with crippling effect.

Noise may be the worst problem, anyone who has heard a multi-engined jet at close range may conclude. But it's a problem with solutions already at hand.

To kill the low roar that comes from the tailpipes, all jets that are on order will come equipped with noise suppressors. These devices, which smooth the turbulence of exhaust gases that drive the planes, will depress the noise level on takeoff to below that of today's biggest planes. This may please the people who live near the airports, but it is costly. American Airlines estimates the price tag on each suppressor—one per engine—at around $37,000. Besides, by reducing thrust and adding drag, the gadgets will add about 4 per cent to the fuel bill.

To quiet the short-range whine of the compressors while planes are entering and leaving the loading area may call for remodeling of the terminals. And this problem applies to the turboprop planes as well as the pure jets. The Vickers Viscount, for example, makes an ear-piercing whine while taxiing, and when such planes become more numerous, this sound could be seriously annoying.

Fortunately, the high-frequency whine carries only a few hundred feet and doesn't go around corners without losing its bite. Tests at Boeing Airplane Company show that it can be controlled by enclosing the passenger concourses and by setting up seven-and-a-half-foot blast fences.

American Airlines plans to run its jet airliners into bays that incoporate both blast fences, sound-tight passenger concourses, and enclosed gangways. Ground crewmen working in exposed places will have to wear ear muffs or helmets. The fences will keep the noise from one plane from bothering service crews at adjacent stations.

United Airlines is also talking about protecting its passengers' ears by soundproofing the walkways. Trans World Airlines is making its $12 million modernistic terminal at Idlewild adaptable enough so it could use whatever system turns out to be best.

Of course, airport operators aren't looking happily toward the day when they will have to air-condition these passageways as well as waiting rooms.

Spick-and-span housekeeping of runways and aprons becomes more than a matter of pride in the jet age. The Air Force has found that the path of jets must be meticulously swept, to keep bits of gravel and stray metal from whisking into jet intakes and ripping engines apart.

Now, the civilian airports will have to be equipped with king-sized vacuum cleaners to protect the jets. . . .

There may be changes, too, in how the jet airliners are handled on the ground. That's largely because of their thirst for fuel. A typical new jet will burn as much fuel per minute while idling on the ground as a DC-7 burns while in the air. American Airlines calculates it will cost $2.50 for each minute a jet spends taxiing or sitting at the head of the runway. That's at a fuel consumption rate of seven hundred gallons an hour.

Ever since jets were first discussed and their fuel rates were figured, experts have been predicting ways that the airlines would save fuel. For instance, an incoming jet liner could cut off its engines the moment it stopped rolling, then wait for a tractor-tug to haul it to the terminal.

It now appears that the airlines won't adopt this tactic, mostly because it's such an ignominiously slow way for a 600-mile-per-hour jet to travel the last lap of its journey to the unloading gate. Most airlines say they plan to taxi the jets both in and out of their parking stations on the apron. One exception is American, which will taxi the planes in, head-on to the terminal, but tow them back out and turn them around by tractor. This has the advantage of saving parking space; with no need for room for the pilot to pivot the plane under its own power, each plane will need only about 190 feet instead of 220 feet.

One way the lines will save fuel is to leave their jet planes loaded at the terminal until the control tower clears them for takeoff. Then they'll start the engines, taxi directly into takeoff. This saves minutes of idling at the start of the runway, where pilots now ask the tower for clearance.

Of course, when takeoffs are delayed by traffic or weather, parking space at the gates may be needed before the loaded planes get their all-clear. In such cases, the airlines plan to move them to nearby waiting spots and shut down the engines again, except for one idling to supply electricity.

Bad weather could also trouble the incoming jet liners more than today's piston-driven planes. The new planes will burn fuel fast enough at their designed cruising altitude of 30,000 to 35,000 feet. As they descend, they burn fuel faster until at sea level they consume 20 per cent more. So they could use up their reserves at a great rate if they were forced to circle for long at low altitudes.

Nevertheless, the latest word is that jets won't get priorities over older types in landing. They'll have to carry reserves of fuel in the same ratio as present planes; they'll have to take their turn landing. The only concession planned will be to stack them at 20,000 feet upward instead of only a few thousand feet. When they get clearance to land, they will dive fast, relying on dive brakes—the first ever fitted on American airliners (the French Caravelle uses them)—to check their speed for touchdown.

Airlines are also campaigning for better weather reporting, so jets won't waste time going to a closed-in field or circling in vain to wait for it to open.

Keeping Them Moving

The whole business of handling the passengers on the ground —from the making of reservations to the loading of people and luggage—is the field where improvements would pay off most handsomely as a competitive advantage. . . . Most airline officials will admit that improvements are overdue, even without the prospect of jets.

That's one reason the new $29 million International Arrival Building . . . [which opened at Idlewild in November 1957] contains such a feature as a sixty-four-aisle supermarket-type checkout stand for getting passengers quickly through Customs. Today's planes carry so many people that baggage-claim and Customs facilities are periodically overloaded. The jets will bring still bigger crowds, as many as 150 at a time.

Both from their own standpoint and that of the travelers, the airlines see more pressure to keep the planes moving. The jets represent an investment of around $6 million apiece, and they earn money only when they're flying. Meanwhile, their speed—for instance, one and a half hours from Chicago to New York—will make any delays on the ground doubly aggravating to riders.

For faster loading and unloading, the jets will have a door at each end of the cabin. United and American will go a step further by eliminating the mobile stairs, loading and unloading instead from the second floor of the terminal. . . . TWA hasn't committed itself on second-level loading, but it is planning to use moving sidewalks to carry passengers through the plane-loading concourses. Some lines, including American, expect to preload baggage in bins to speed up this phase of the operations, too.

Preloading of passengers is also the idea of Clark Equipment Company with its "Passenger Pod" system of taking people to and from planes remote from the waiting room. These detachable, bus-like units carry forty to sixty passengers and cost $6,000 to $8,000 each. As airports grow in acreage and the jets produce more problems on the ground, interest in such systems is expected to grow.

Meanwhile, the airlines expect to cut a plane's turnaround time to half an hour by moving passengers on and off at one level while the servicing goes on at ground level. Gasoline trucks may be replaced by underground hydrants with high-pressure systems that can load the fuel tanks at 1,700 gallons a minute.

Philadelphia's Division of Aviation proposes a system to haul planes around airports on rail flatcars. A built-in rail system connecting each gate position with the ends of the runways would carry the jets back and forth without using their engines. They could even be fueled and serviced while being piggy-backed on the rail cars; they wouldn't be making any noise near the terminal. . . . Cost is estimated at $150,000 per gate position.

Even with conventional ways of moving planes around airports, the jets look like a formidable problem. They will weigh 250,000 to 300,000 pounds, which is about all any ordinary airport tractor can pull. When the pavement is wet or icy, towing gets still harder.

Bigger tugs are being groomed for the job of towing jets. They'll weigh fifteen to twenty tons and be priced at about a dollar a pound. . . . Clark Equipment, which claims it sells most of the airport tractors nowadays, plans a supersized model.

Other manufacturers favor a different approach. They plan to use the weight of the airliner itself to give traction as they apply power to the plane's own landing wheels . . . by clamping a powered wheel against a landing wheel tire, turning it by friction.

JETS ACROSS THE SEA [4]

The international airlines are preparing for the breath-taking potential of jet power with high confidence—a confidence based on their achievements in the brief span that has elapsed since intercontinental flying ceased being an adventure for the few and became a conventional mode of travel for millions. Penetrating into areas scarcely touched by mechanized transport before, they have transformed isolated places like Kano, Nigeria, into great international crossroads. From their postwar start a scant dozen years ago, with motley fleets of Dakotas and Skymasters that had been built for the military, the airlines have become the premier means of transportation between nations.

Last year the eighty-four airlines that belong to the International Air Transport Association, and that handle more than 85 per cent of all international traffic, flew 1.3 billion miles on domestic and intercontinental routes connecting some 3,500 cities, carried 65 million passengers, 270 million ton-miles of mail, and 830 million ton-miles of cargo. Since 1946, when they began their postwar surge, their total traffic has increased fivefold.

The only trouble with all this is profits. Last year the eighty-four international airlines netted a grand total of only $50 million, or little better than 1 per cent of total revenue. This is not a robust condition for an industry that is about to buy a great deal of brand-new equipment and take on a great many brand-new operating problems. The airlines must pay a staggering bill for their new planes and a no less imposing one for the new auxiliary

[4] From "International Airlines: The Great Jet Gamble." *Fortune.* 67:120-4+. Reprinted by special permission from the June 1958 issue of *Fortune* magazine. Copyright 1958 by Time Inc.

facilities needed to operate jets safely and efficiently. They will have to replan their schedules, thereby further aggravating the thorny question of rights to fly international routes. They will meet competition from a new quarter, Soviet Russia. And these international airlines will have to find new ways to fill the vastly increased passenger capacity that the jet age will afford them.

Within the next four years the world's civilian air fleet will be augmented by 914 new planes that will cost $2.8 billion, almost as much as the aggregate worth of all the planes now flying. A thick slice of these orders is destined for the highly developed United States domestic air system, but almost half the orders have been placed by foreign carriers, and a majority of the new planes will fly on international routes. Despite the fact that they are more than twice as costly as any plane now flying, 285 giant Boeing 707's and Douglas DC-8's, worth in all more than $1.5 billion, are on order, and their purchasers include at least sixteen foreign airlines. Also due for delivery by 1961 are about $500 million worth of smaller jets: Britain's DeHavilland Comet 4, France's Caravelle, the United States Convair 880 and Boeing 720.

The airlines hope to meet part of the stiff purchase price of their new fleets by trading in old planes. Through most of the postwar years the used-aircraft market has been brisk, and resales have helped greatly to ease the expense of reequipment. But the change-over to jets will be so rapid and widespread that there is bound to be a glut of discarded DC-7's and Constellations. There are signs already that the secondhand market is collapsing.

The price tag on the jets is only the beginning of the outlays the airlines will be called on to make. IATA Director-General Sir William Hildred summed up the prospects in his latest annual report:

> One does not buy a $5 million jet as if it were a new bicycle. Even one jet aircraft necessitates special maintenance facilities, maybe a new base or a new hangar, extensive training of ground and airborne personnel, complete replanning of ground handling facilities, and many other changes in airline organization, all of which begin costing money before the aircraft can be put into service . . . I should not be surprised if the secondary expense of putting jets into operation were in the long run equal to their original purchase price." . . .

Until the jets actually fly on regular schedules, little will be known for certain about their operating costs. The best guess is that if they are flown with utmost precision, at optimum altitude, and without diversions or delays once they have started up their engines, their per-mile cost of operation will be not much greater than that for piston planes. But taking into account the high initial cost and the considerable cost of the additional auxiliary services, they will be an extravagance unless they are flown many hours every day, their cabins well filled with paying customers. Operators are aiming for a fully loaded round-trip transatlantic flight each day per plane.

These factors are bound to create much hotter competition on long-distance, high-density routes, such as the North Atlantic and Latin American runs, where the jets can pick up enough traffic to keep flying almost continually with profitable payloads. But the very advantage of the intercontinental jets—their ability to complete many more flights in a given time and carry many more passengers on each—may break some carriers that plan to operate with them. A fully employed Boeing 707 can transport the same load as twenty Dakotas, nine Skymasters, or five Constellations in any stated period, and over the course of a year can match the *Queen Mary* in total passengers carried. Unless there is a sudden tremendous expansion of traffic, therefore, the introduction of jets will mean that fewer planes will be needed. In fact, when Pan Am puts its Boeings into service next autumn, one daily flight to Paris will replace two piston flights on its winter European schedule. . . .

The coming of the jets, in other words, may force many of the smaller lines out of the big-time competition. But some countries whose flag carriers are now flying prestige routes halfway around the world could instead profitably beef up their domestic systems to improve their internal communications. A few small airlines may find a way to stay in fast company by pooling resources, as the Norwegians, Swedes, and Danes did twelve years ago in setting up the now formidable SAS.

Express Routes and Milk Runs

Today transatlantic carriers offer direct flights from New York to a dozen or so European cities, with each airline continuing on eastward across the Continent in four-hundred- or five-hundred-mile hops. In the jet age they are likely to put the big planes on nonstop express services back and forth between New York and four main centers: London, Paris, Frankfurt, and Rome. There passengers will transfer to smaller aircraft for their final destination. Jets will in time take over the busier milk-run routes too, but they will be smaller ones like the French Caravelle, the British Comet, and Boeing's scaled-down 720. United States transatlantic operators will want to maintain their own through services to many cities in Europe so that they can carry long-distance passengers not only across the ocean but to their ultimate destinations. Similarly, European carriers will seek to continue services into the center of the United States as well as to New York.

The new route patterns will put a strain on the delicate web of diplomatic agreements that make it possible for airlines to operate internationally. Beginning with the 1946 Bermuda Agreement with Britain, the United States has negotiated some fifty of these pacts. On the basis of fair exchange, the United States concedes a foreign-flag carrier the privilege of landing and doing business in certain American cities, in return for which United States airlines gain the right to operate through routes in the country of the foreign carrier.

In place of complete freedom of the air, which the United States unsuccessfully espoused at the end of the war, international route agreements recognize and define "five freedoms." The first is the freedom to fly over a foreign country without landing; the second, to land for refueling. These are recognized as unlimited rights by most nations outside the Soviet bloc. The other three freedoms are negotiable between individual nations. The third allows one country the right to carry passengers abroad to a foreign country; the fourth, to bring passengers back from that foreign country. The fifth freedom allows an airline to pick up passengers abroad who are bound for other foreign points: i.e., a United States carrier to pick up travelers in London for Frankfurt or Zurich or Rome. The measure of fifth freedom to be granted is usually the point of contention in route agreements.

United States route agreements with foreign countries are negotiated by the State Department, which was appointed bargaining agent by the Civil Aeronautics Act of 1938. The department's job in negotiating is to combine high-policy considerations and domestic economic aims. On the latter it is guided by airline demands and by the Civil Aeronautics Board, which is the arbiter of where United States airlines will fly. In one recent instance, high policy overruled economics: last year's agreement with the Netherlands government, defining rights for KLM.

The Dutch airline, which had been flying between Amsterdam and New York and between Curaçao and Miami, wanted to open a route to the West Coast plus a Curaçao-New York route. United States carriers vehemently opposed this request, arguing that the United States could not get in return anything commensurate with the advantages that would accrue to the Dutch. Queen Juliana and her ministers made it virtually an issue of national honor and economic survival, and the State Department, in the interests of good relations with an ally, gave KLM a compromised version of what it wanted. Curaçao-New York was granted, but instead of the West Coast run, KLM got Houston.

As might be expected, the State Department is accused at home of following a "giveaway philosophy" that lets foreign airlines siphon off traffic in territory United States operators would like to consider their own preserve. They complain that lines operated by the Scandinavians, Dutch, Belgians, and others, whose own population centers have little potentiality for greater development by American airlines, are being allowed to expand their "fifth freedom" operations in the United States. Pan Am and TWA say that their combined share of the North Atlantic traffic is steadily dwindling. Indeed, it declined from 57 per cent in 1951 to 49 last year, but in the same period Pan Am's actual passenger total tripled and TWA's doubled.

On the other flank, the State Department is assailed by foreign lines that want even easier access to United States cities. Air France, for instance, is clamoring to be allowed on the polar route to California, which SAS pioneered so successfully and which Pan Am and TWA too are now happily exploiting. In dealing with these demands, State is not helped by the intensifying protectionist attitude of United States carriers. As former Deputy Assistant Secretary of State Thorsten V. Kalijarvi put it not long ago:

> If we want to continue aviation relations with other countries, we cannot prevent foreign carriers from serving major population centers in the United States just because their countries do not have points of equal traffic-generating importance. . . . Restriction only leads to counter-restriction.

The State Department would like to have United States carriers stop crying over the loss of their onetime near-monopoly position in the United States market and look ahead to the new problems that will be brought on by the jet age. The danger, as some officials see it, is that while United States carriers bicker about past grievances, real or fancied, they will find themselves in the jet age without the rights to fly where and when they need to in order to make their new equipment pay off. . . .

Lingua Franca of the Air

Notwithstanding all the high and low politics of the international air, the ordinary passenger can travel thousands of miles without being aware that international rivalry plays any part in the business. A Greek in Salonika who wants to fly to New York with business stopovers en route, can walk into the local office of Olympic Airways and book a through ticket that takes him to Athens on Olympic, to Rome on Alitalia, to London on BEA, and across the Atlantic on Pan Am. And he can plunk down drachmas in Salonika to pay for the whole thing.

Although individual airlines are dedicated to battling grimly for national prestige and their own profit, international air travel has been integrated into one unified system, in which pilots, radiomen, control-tower personnel, and ticket salesmen, wherever they may be and whomever they work for, use the same procedures, communicate with each other in the same terminology, and in fact usually the same language, for English has become the lingua franca of the international airways. What makes this possible are two international agencies, both based in Montreal—one, ICAO, an organization of governments; the other, IATA [International Air Transport Association] to which airlines belong. ICAO, the International Civil Aviation Organization, is a UN affiliate that seventy-two nations (not including the Soviet Union) have joined. Its threefold function is to disseminate new aviation ideas originating with individual members, to carry on its own technical research for the benefit of airline operators, and to recommend safety standards and operating methods to which all nations with airlines can adhere.

IATA's emblem of success is the fully negotiable airline ticket, which is honored everywhere except in the Soviet bloc. Pan Am is perfectly willing to honor the ticket sold to the Salonika traveler by Olympic because of a unique banking institution, the IATA Clearing House—two men and a girl in a tiny London office—through which member airlines settle their accounts with each other. Instead of billing each other separately, they report once a month to the Clearing House what is owing them. The staff totes one debt against another, like the banker in a poker game, and cancels them out where possible. In the end the only cash that changes hands is from the Clearing House to net creditor airlines and to the Clearing House from net debtors. Payment can be made in either dollars or sterling. Last year the Clearing House processed $639,249,000 worth of accounts, settling only 11.1 per cent in cash.

IATA also acts as price fixer. Meeting under its auspices in three regional conferences, usually held once a year, airline representatives set the fares to be charged on all routes. Decisions must be unanimous and are subject to approval by all governments concerned. Violators are liable to fines. The deliberate aim is to eliminate cutthroat competition such as might develop if a heavily subsidized airline tried to corner a market. Though United States lines participate in the price fixing, they are not enthusiastic about it. So that the practice could be exempted from United States antitrust acts, the CAB insisted on the safeguard of government veto power.

Since their inception, IATA fare conferences have been a struggle between two philosophies: one that is expansionist and predominantly American, pressing for lower airline costs and rock-bottom fares to attract volume traffic; the other, a restrictionist and generally European view, fearful that reduced fares will bring mounting losses.

The low-fare advocates scored their first victory in 1951 when the Atlantic Conference set up tourist class, 30 per cent cheaper than the previous standard rate (which became first class), with seats narrowed to a maximum of thirty-nine inches so more passengers could be packed into a cabin, simpler food, and no free drinks. (Current tourist summer rate for the New York-Paris round trip is $603.) It was just the stimulus needed to keep up the momentum of the initial postwar traffic boom. Within five years . . . [the tourist class] doubled North Atlantic traffic. Almost from its inception two thirds of all passengers have traveled tourist.

Trouble arose when the airlines didn't leave tourist as simple and basic as it was intended to be. They kept adding frills and then, to maintain the differential, embellished first class with new luxuries. "Five years ago," says a United States airline executive, "we served braised beef on tourist flights. Now braised beef has given way to roast beef." As for first class, a CAB official notes that "we've even got to the point where one carrier was getting 'em drunk on the ground *before* they poured 'em into the airplane." Inevitably costs rose, building up pressure for a fare increase. The cut-fare advocates pleaded anew for stripped-down service and still cheaper tickets.

The clash came to a climax in the 1955 IATA Atlantic Conference, which agreed to raise the first-class fare 10 per cent and leave tourist unchanged. Disapprovingly, CAB commented: "The appropriate corrective action at this time was not an increase . . . but a basic realignment of services so as to exploit efficiently the reasonable maximum capabilities of modern aircraft." On the board's urging, the Atlantic Conference went back into session. Finally it agreed in principle to adopt Pan Am's proposal for a North Atlantic economy fare, 20 per cent lower than tourist, or $489.60 for the summer New York-Paris round trip. Another full-dress meeting was needed to get agreement on details: i.e., five inches less seat room in economy than in tourist and only sandwiches as refreshment. Under economy specifications, it became possible, for the first time, to pack more than one hundred people into a plane for a long-distance trip. In effect since April 1 of this year, economy has already been phenomenally successful. Pan Am expects it to add 300,000 passengers to the transatlantic total this year.

The economy fare came along just in time to provide international airlines with a badly needed antidote against the recession. In . . . [the first quarter of 1958], business retrenchment and the consequent falling off of expense-account traffic hit the airlines badly. KLM, for instance, lost $1,788,000, Pan Am about $3 million, and TWA a shattering $11,063,000. This summer, thanks to the economy booster, increased tourist traffic should win back some of these losses.

Economy class is rapidly crowding out tourist (SAS has already abandoned it) because no one wants to pay $100 for an extra five inches of seat. When the jets shorten the transatlantic hop to six and a half hours and the premium on luxury recedes even further, first class could become an airborne version of the genteel but anachronistic railroad parlor car.

Battle of the Sandwiches

But in economy class, just as it had been with tourist, some airlines couldn't let simplicity alone. The lowly sandwich, symbol of minimal sustenance, began to be aggrandized. When Pan Am's efficient espionage service detected that some of the European lines were piling whole rich meals of paté, fish, and even fruit on a slice of bread and calling it a sandwich, it indignantly hauled Air France, KLM, SAS, and Swissair before IATA's "Breaches Committee." The furious legal-culinary skirmish that ensued has gone down in history as "the battle of the sandwiches." IATA's decision, handed down by no less a personage than its director-general, was wordy but definitive:

Each sandwich to be a separate unit, the whole meal not to give the appearance of a cold plate. A substantial and visible part of each unit to consist of bread, rolls, or similar breadlike material. . . . Each unit to be simple, that is, not complicated. . . . This calls for a minimum of garnishing. Each unit to be inexpensive. This calls for the avoidance of materials normally regarded as expensive or luxurious, such as . . . smoked salmon, oysters, caviar, lobster, game . . .

"The battle of the sandwiches" was not just a clash between cuisines. It was a symptom of the strain of competing in a price-regulated setting. An airline is told where it can fly and how much it can charge. Though a carrier can gain a temporary advantage by introducing a new plane (for example, BEA with the Viscount in Europe), eventually its rivals catch up and everyone is offering the same plane, the same flight time. Safety has been internationalized, too. Practically everybody, down to the smallest bush line, observes the recommendations of ICAO. The average passenger now assumes all lines will get him to his destination more or less on schedule. He is looking for something else, and what it is is pretty elusive. Airlines are spending a lot of money, time, and energy trying to provide this special something. . . .

The coming of the jets is not going to do away with the need for ordinary salesmanship, but salesmanship alone will not appease the airlines' hunger for traffic. Four years from now, when all the new planes now on order have been delivered, capacity of the international lines will be doubled. For the past five years international traffic has been growing at an annual rate of 15 per cent, nothing to be ashamed of, but hardly sufficient to fill the seats that will be available in the early 1960's. Only a new boom in travel will accomplish that, and the only reliable means of bringing it about is a new assault on the level of fares. As IATA's Sir William Hildred says, "Lower the height of the dam even a very little, and millions of gallons of water will flow over."

Oddly enough, Hildred's point has been proved by a tiny airline that refuses to take IATA's fare dictation. Icelandic Airlines, by operating old DC-4's and minimizing overhead, manages to offer a transatlantic round trip, from New York to Oslo, for $472.20, or $50 less than anyone else. With a minimum of promotional fanfare it has built up a clientele of 25,000 passengers a year, most of them, according to an Icelandic executive, "people who hitherto simply could not afford to travel by air."

The Profit Squeeze

The resistance of other lines to lower fares is usually based on the fact that costs are rising. Like every other industry, international airlines have had to struggle with inflation. They have had to pay more for their fuel and parts, and their salary bills have risen relentlessly. But for a time they did better than most industries, largely because they were able to keep productivity rising faster than costs. This was not difficult at first. Most airlines started with a miscellany of equipment, haphazard ground facilities, and sketchy organization. Simply tightening up all around worked wonders. Bigger planes, quicker turnaround, fewer expensive refueling stops—these helped even more. But as the room for obvious improvement narrowed, profits began to slip. In the past three years the international airlines' total operating profit has dwindled alarmingly. In 1955 they grossed $3.025 billion and made a profit of $78 million or 2.6 per cent. In 1956 they grossed $3.51 billion and their profit was $84 million or 2.5 per cent. Then in 1957, though revenues rose above $4 billion, profit, as already noted, fell to $50 million, or barely more than 1 per cent.

These figures would look even worse were it not for the government largess on which some airlines rely. About half of all international airlines are government owned; wholly private ones are rare outside the United States. The degree of government control varies widely. Some lines are government-owned corporations like BOAC and BEA, which are, however, quite independent in making their own policy. In others there is a substantial government equity, as in KLM, 71.7 per cent the property of the Dutch Government. In all cases where governments are involved, it can be taken for granted that they will meet any deficits that arise.

Even with the privately owned airlines, governments are liberal with handouts. Subsidies are, in most cases, deliberately concealed and hard to pin down. They can take the form of financing new equipment, training pilots gratis, giving fat contracts for carrying government personnel, paying mail fees above the going rate. Fortunately, subsidy is becoming a bad word in airline circles (Pan Am has been off subsidy since October 1956; TWA since 1952), but it is still too early to say that the industry as a whole is ready to stand on its own financial feet.

When the jet bills begin coming in, the government cushion won't provide much comfort. For an airline that can't make a go of it, the deficits will mount so fast that taxpayers, no matter how proud they are of having their flag flown around the world, are not likely to put up with the cost.

The only answer to the cost problem is greater volume. The great potentials are staring everyone in the face. One is air freight, which is no longer limited to small-packaged, exotic, and perishable luxury items. Enterprising lines like Seaboard & Western, the only all-cargo carrier crossing the Atlantic, have developed a profitable business shipping textiles, sports cars, and race horses. As for passengers, in the United States, despite the phenomenal rise in the general standard of living and income level, international travel is still considered a luxury for the few. Surveys show that only .6 per cent of the population has ever traveled abroad at all, that a large majority of airline passengers are in professional, managerial, and technical occupations, that the average tourist flying to Europe makes $10,000 a year and has more than four weeks to spend abroad. Says Willis G. Lipscomb, Pan Am's vice president for traffic and sales:

Orchids, champagne, and *pâté de foie gras* won't sell us to the man who's spending his two-weeks-with-pay in Miami. We've got to convince him that foreign travel is within his means. We ought to be thinking in terms of a $300 round trip to Europe.

THE SHAPE OF THINGS TO COME [5]

As the aircraft industry enters the second decade of supersonic flight, it is trying, paradoxically, to devise machines that can

[5] From "VTOL: The Next Way to Fly," article by Francis Bello, associate editor of *Fortune*. *Fortune*. 57:136-7+. Reprinted by special permission from the March 1958 issue of *Fortune* magazine. Copyright 1958 by Time Inc.

stand still while flying. The objective: to produce a new breed of VTOL (vertical takeoff and landing) aircraft that can outperform the slow-moving helicopter. Some experimental VTOL machines are merely jet engines rigged up so they will balance on their own exhaust; others switch from vertical to horizontal flight by tilting engines, propellers, or whole wings; a third group hovers or shoots forward by deflection of the propeller slip-stream or jet exhaust.

The new VTOL and STOL (short takeoff and landing) aircraft should arrive just in time to overcome what some experts are calling the "runway barrier." The new jet transports, the Douglas DC-8 and the Boeing 707, will approach airports at about 150 miles per hour and use up nearly a mile of runway after they have touched down. For takeoff, Federal regulations will confine the new planes to runways that are at least a mile and a half long, and these are none too plentiful. Moreover, with their high fuel consumption, the new jets will be penalized by the fact that airports cannot permit more than one large transport to land at a time. If takeoffs and landings could be made vertically, or nearly so, the capacity of the nation's airports would be vastly multiplied, and the threefold expansion in traffic anticipated by 1970 could be handled with a minimum of new construction.

The United States appears to have a substantial lead in the VTOL field although considerable work is being done abroad. . . . While all the VTOL aircraft announced so far in the United States have been research vehicles, Bell Aircraft is known to be designing a supersonic VTOL fighting machine for the Navy and Air Force. Details of the machine are classified, but it will probably achieve vertical flight by using vanes to deflect the exhaust of its jet engine downward, following the principle that Bell was the first to demonstrate in its X-14.

Bell engineers predict that within the next ten to fifteen years VTOL transports flying at twice the speed of sound (Mach 2) will be ready for commercial use. This optimistic view is shared by a special committee that last year recommended to the Air League of the British Empire that British industry develop a VTOL transport capable of crossing the Atlantic in two or three hours—"a practical proposition within the next ten years."

In some respects, the most remarkable VTOL vehicles under development are what the Army calls "Flying Jeeps." Entirely wingless, the proposed jeeps will be the closest thing yet to a flying carpet. They will be lifted off the ground and driven forward by horizontal propellers or fans buried within the machine. With no more horsepower than a modern automobile, the jeep should be able to hoist itself straight up and outrace a car in forward speed. It may be the first flying machine that can be converted into a practical family vehicle that can take off and land in the backyard.

The Jet-Propelled Bootstrap

The development that cleared the way for the wide-scale exploration of vertical flight was the gas-turbine engine. In turboprop form it can produce up to three horsepower for each pound of its own weight; as a pure jet engine it can produce five to eight pounds of thrust per pound of weight. The old reciprocating engine can produce barely one horsepower per pound. At that power-to-weight ratio, the airplane was fated to remain nothing more than a souped-up glider in which lift was produced by the flow of air over a suitably shaped wing. Even the most powerful propeller-driven fighting planes of World War II were never quite able to support their own weight and keep climbing when pointed directly skyward.

Vertical flight with the reciprocating engine became possible only with the advent of the helicopter in the late thirties. In this device the rotor, which is actually a rotating wing, finally achieved what the simple propeller could not: it produced the required multiplication of engine thrust needed for vertical takeoff and landing. The deficiencies of the helicopter are well known: it has limited forward speed (present record: 162 miles per hour), limited range and payload, and it is costly to build and maintain. While range and payload are being improved in new models powered by gas turbines, the helicopter can never reach the speeds demanded for many jobs, both military and civilian.

The Air Force and Navy began looking for new VTOL devices that would outperform the helicopter at about the same time, around 1948. . . . Designing a VTOL machine is a severe test of the aeronautical engineer's skill in reaching compromises. In a VTOL device the characteristics that favor high speed are antithetical to a high efficiency in takeoff and hovering. The most efficient vertical-lifting mechanism yet discovered is the helicopter rotor, for it moves a large volume of air relatively slowly. One of the least efficient lifters is the exhaust of a jet engine. For every minute of hovering flight, a jet VTOL machine will consume ten to twenty times as much fuel as a helicopter of the same weight. The other VTOL types fall between these extremes in hovering efficiency.

About three years ago, to narrow down the number of VTOL alternatives, the Office of Naval Research asked a number of aircraft firms to recommend designs for VTOL military transports that could be flying operationally by 1960. . . . This is how the three VTOL concepts, all using turboprops, were divided up:

The tilting-wing approach is being pursued by Vertol of Morton, Pennsylvania, and by Hiller of Palo Alto. The Vertol craft, the smaller of the two, is finished and has successfully hovered, but at this writing has not "translated" from hovering to forward flight. Hiller's X-18, the first transport-size VTOL to be built in the United States, is near completion. . . .

The deflected-slipstream aircraft are being built by Ryan, and by Fairchild, Hagerstown, Maryland. In these planes the propeller slipstream is forced to curve downward, at takeoff, by large retractable flaps along the rear of the wing. The Ryan Vertiplane was completed last winter; the Fairchild craft is still under construction.

Both the tilting-wing and the deflected-slipstream machines should perform especially well as VTOL aircraft. A short takeoff run will permit them to get off the ground with substantially greater loads than they can lift straight up.

The tilting ducted-propeller scheme is being followed by Doak Aircraft of Torrance, California.

With present technology, these three types of VTOL aircraft appear to be closely competitive both in speed and in payload capacity. All should yield transport vehicles capable of flying at

300 to 450 miles per hour. And while studies made by Vertol show that the tilt wing may carry a slightly greater payload than the other two types, the differences appear slight enough so that the competition may well be decided by comparative ease of handling, safety, simplicity, and ruggedness.

Twisting the Jet's Tail

For flight much above 400 miles per hour VTOL designers must switch to pure jet propulsion. Perhaps the greatest enthusiasts for VTOL jet flight are to be found at Bell Aircraft, builder of the first airplane to exceed the speed of sound.

Back when Bell was building its first helicopter, in 1941, it applied for a patent, subsequently issued, on a VTOL tail-sitter of the Pogo type. Since then, Bell engineers have become convinced that to be practical a VTOL machine must take off and land in a normal horizontal attitude.

In 1953, without military financing, Bell began putting together a primitive "VTOL air-test vehicle." The vehicle's two jet engines, looking like garbage cans, were suspended on the sides of the fuselage and could be rotated from a vertical position, for takeoff and landing, to a horizontal position, for forward flight.

For its first "flights," the air test vehicle was rigged up with safety cables to see how stably it would hover while balanced on its own exhaust. In November 1954, Bell test pilot David W. Howe hovered successfully without tethers. In May 1955, Howe finally carried out the tricky business of rotating the engines from horizontal to vertical and back, while in flight.

Bell engineers had meanwhile begun studying the feasibility of deflecting the jet exhaust downward instead of tilting the entire engine. The big problem was to design a deflection system that would turn the hot jet gases through an angle of ninety degrees without sacrificing more than a few per cent of engine thrust. Many engineers doubted that this could be done.

Bell nevertheless received an Air Force contract to build an experimental deflected-thrust jet aircraft known as the X-14, and in February 1957 the machine hovered successfully. It is the success of these two jet-propelled VTOL machines that has made Bell so bullish about the commercial future of VTOL flight. "If aircraft history tells us anything," says George Ray, chief engineer of Bell's aircraft division, "it is that almost every prediction made in this industry has been too conservative." . . .

If there is anyone more visionary in this field than Bell engineers it is probably Alexander M. Lippisch, formerly a top designer for Messerschmitt and credited with the world's first rocket-powered fighter, the delta-wing Me-163. Since 1950, Lippisch has been head of the Aeronautical Research Laboratory of Collins Radio Company, Cedar Rapids, Iowa.

With Collins support and intermittent backing from ONR, Lippisch has built a series of flying models of what he calls the "Aerodyne"—"a wingless aircraft which produces its lift and propulsion from one common source of energy through an internal flow system." The Aerodyne, in short, is a pure thrust deflecter. Depending on the speed desired, the thrust may be obtained from ducted propellers or fans, or, for supersonic speeds, from jet engines.

Wings: Who Needs Them?

Lippisch maintains that aircraft engineers have remained too long in the thrall of wings because they provide an important measure of safety in event of power failure. Lippisch proposes to achieve comparable safety by using many engines and making them accessible for in-flight repairs. For the stability that is now provided by wings, he would substitute completely electronic stabilization of the thrust mechanism, which explains why an electronics manufacturer is pleased to support his research. The advantage of eliminating all wings, of course, is that they represent the major source of drag in high-speed aircraft. So, says Lippisch, off with wings. . . .

The Army's Flying Jeeps are being designed without wings not to reduce drag but because wings would just be in the way and add nothing to performance.

Lieutenant General James M. Gavin, . . . [former] chief of Army Research and Development, has quipped that the Flying Jeep should be described technically as "a zero ground pressure vehicle," reflecting the fact that the Army is not interested in getting very high off the ground. It just wants to get up high enough so it can move swiftly across rivers, marshes, and rugged country, seeking cover in the "nap of the earth" wherever possible. Army officers speak enthusiastically of the aerial jeep's bringing back the mobility advantage that the horse cavalry gave land forces in the old days.

Last summer the Army gave out contracts for building prototypes of the Flying Jeep to three firms: Piasecki Aircraft, Aerophysics Development (a subsidiary of Curtiss-Wright), and Chrysler. . . .

The formidable assignment given to the three firms is to build a vehicle weighing about 1,500 pounds that will be able to lift a useful load of 1,000 pounds, or roughly 65 per cent of its own weight. Whether any of the prototypes can achieve this goal seems doubtful, however, since even with the help of wings, few small aircraft can lift more than half of their weight in useful load. . . .

Much of the basic research on the manifold problems of VTOL flight has been done at the Langley Aeronautical Laboratory of the National Advisory Committee for Aeronautics. The engineer in charge of NACA's VTOL and STOL work is Charles Zimmerman, who, in 1946, built the first one-man "flying platform." The small engines then available were not adequate to permit flight more than a few inches from the ground, but what Zimmerman foresaw is that almost anyone ought to be able to fly such a platform simply by shifting his weight instinctively, using his natural sense of balance. This is called "kinesthetic control" and is the control method used in the Hiller "Flying Platform." Hiller made a major advance on Zimmerman's original concept by placing the propeller within a shroud or duct, which enhances the propeller's lifting capacity some 20 to 30 per cent. The Hiller machine was first flown without safety cables in April 1955 and gave the Army the idea for the Flying Jeep.

A New Lease for the Wing

Another NACA interest is one that promises to transform the aircraft wing as greatly as the gas turbine transformed the power plant. It is a new principle that can multiply the lifting power of aircraft wings by a factor of four or five. The principle, in various modifications, is called the jet-augmented flap, the jet flap, or the jet wing. While it will not enable an aircraft to rise vertically or hover, it should lead to high-speed jet planes that can take off and land in less than one tenth of the distance required by the DC-8 and the 707.

To produce the jet-wing effect, the entire exhaust blast from the plane's jet engines must be forced to flow in a thin sheet over a flap that extends across the entire trailing edge of the wing. In a normal flight, when the flap is horizontal, the jet stream creates a normal forward thrust. When the flap is tilted downward during the takeoff and landing, however, the high-velocity sheet of gas also tilts downward, thereby producing a great multiplication in the lifting power of the wing. The effect is dramatic. . . .

The jet wing presents a number of new problems in aircraft design, the biggest being how to construct flaps that will stand up to the jet engine's fiery exhaust, but the NACA believes that solutions are in sight.

If the jet wing works out as expected, it will probably lead to a major revision in aircraft design: the main wing may be forced back to the tail of the aircraft and a small wing, resembling the present stabilizer, may have to be shifted forward to the craft's nose. Aircraft engineers refer to this as a "canard" design since it suggests a duck in flight. Such a configuration would take maximum advantage of the jet wing's high lifting power.

Following the pattern established in the earliest days of powered flight, VTOL and STOL aircraft are being developed in response to military need. Fortunately, what the military would like today, the civilian can often use tomorrow. But military and civilian requirements do not wholly coincide, of course, and there is growing room for doubt that the most useful and efficient commercial aircraft will inevitably emerge from military experimenting. . . .

In the years ahead the United States can expect both Britain and Russia to challenge American leadership in commercial aviation even more vigorously than now. For the United States to maintain its historic lead it may have to support, for the first time, a major research and development effort that gives primacy to commercial rather than to military requirements.

THE NEXT FIFTY YEARS [6]

The leading lights of some of our great aircraft companies predict aviation in the year 2000 with a strange mixture of conservatism and, to a layman, fantasy.

Unlike the scientist, they do not finger their slide rules and base their predictions on the probable increments to present knowledge. But they, too, have a measure by which they judge the future.

That measure, is, "How much do you want it?"

"Aviation," they say in effect, "can produce anything that people will buy."

All of them are bothered by the zooming, astronomical cost of aircraft and aircraft research. They feel that, unless we maintain a high level of military spending to pay for research, aviation in this country will develop more slowly than in the past fifty years.

Since they have been stung often by costs rising way beyond estimates, by the hot and cold extremes of war contracts, by booms and busts in the commercial transport field, by numerous unsuccessful ventures into the business of making a private plane that will replace the automobile—for all these reasons the experts agree vehemently on one crucial question mark about aviation's future: Who will pay the cost? . . .

For the highly populated runs the maximum [distance] is 3,000 miles [says J. V. Naish, executive vice president of Convair]. That's coast to coast and continent to continent. The 4,500- and 6,000-mile trips will never be economically feasible to create a whole new method of transportation. There won't be that much traffic density. So if you're talking about a 3,000-mile trip segment, at 1,500 miles an hour, that'd be two hours. If you go to rocketry or something else to reduce it to one hour, the terrific increase in cost would hardly justify it. . . .

[6] From "Aviation's Next Fifty Years: As Industry Sees Them," article by Richard Tregaskis, foreign correspondent and author of *Guadalcanal Diary*. *Nation's Business.* 41:28-9+. Copyright 1953, reprinted from the December 1953 issue of *Nation's Business.*

The Convair No. 1 guided missile expert, J. R. Dempsey, who should know about fantastic speeds, phrases the same proposition in practical language:

Why would you want to go 5,000 miles an hour, if you're going to make a 3,000-mile trip? If you could travel 3,000 miles or so in a couple of hours, that's as fast as you'd want to go in view of what it'd cost you of aviation's future:

Hall Hibbard, Lockheed's vice president in charge of engineering . . . warns aganst being too conservative in prophecies of aviation's future.

I think that if we were to arrive at the year 2000, and look back at what we're saying today, we'd sound like pikers. Because if you go back fifty years ago today, man hadn't even flown—and I can't imagine those fellows fifty years ago looking ahead and saying that we would be roaring around at three hundred miles an hour, carrying people and fighting wars that way. Furthermore there's one thing I'm sure they wouldn't have predicted: that the atom would be conquered as it is today, and that in 1953, we would have practically built an atom-powered engine.

With this perspective, Mr. Hibbard is much more confident than most of the others about the next fifty years in aviation. He feels that the cost factor will be overcome, that possibly atomic energy will increase our national power, and therefore, our financial resources, far beyond the present level—so that we may be able to tackle infinitely greater projects. . . .

Experts agree that the problems of commercial travel beyond the 1,500-mile-per-hour mark, Mach 2 or twice the speed of sound, are too tough to lick without fantastic outlays of money and engineering effort. Apparently, an airplane can fly at speeds up to 1,500 in the earth's atmosphere, but beyond that level the heat generated by air friction gets to be what the engineers mildly call critical; in other words, the aircraft and the people in it just burn up.

One answer would be to fly two hundred miles up out of the earth's atmosphere in our transports, as Hall Hibbard cheerfully predicts. But then we still face the problem of slowing down when we come back to our earth destination.

There are certain definite problems [says Frank Davis of Convair] like getting the thing turned around and stopped. You know it's going to take just as much energy to stop it as it did to get out there. It requires twice as much fuel, of whatever kind you have, to make a round trip back to the earth as the one-way trip. . . .

I think that, at the present rate, we'll go up to probably on the order of 500 or 550 miles an hour and probably remain there for fifteen years at least.

Then I think the next jump will probably be up to the vicinity of 1,000 or 1,500 and we'll probably remain there for some time. . . .

I'm not sure whether the main source of power for transports in the year 2000 will be jet engines or nuclear energy. Probably several kinds of power plants will be flying.

In the matter of private flying, there is no . . . universal agreement among the authorities, although the majority contend that as of the year 2000 the airplane will not have replaced the automobile as the common mode of transport.

The principal objection is traffic discipline.

Mr. Naish sums it up:

As long as gravity is a basic law of physics, you could never build safety into something which is up over the earth's surface. . . . No matter what safety devices we can conjure up, there's no safety device that can keep you safe if you have a head-on collision in the air.

Mr. Davis:

I think two things would stop you: one is safety maintenance for the equipment, which the average person won't do, and the other is traffic discipline. Your penalties for a minor collision are just as high as they are for a major collision. . . .

Says Edgar Schmued [engineering vice president of Northrop] categorically:

The airplane won't be the equivalent of the auto, because of the impossibility of governing traffic as we do on the road. The road is an artery which forces a certain course, and you have a fixed altitude. We could have an electronic device which would steer an airplane away from another. But there are all kinds of messes you could get into. Imagine when you take off from your backyard to go to work; you have to climb up vertically through perhaps two thousand planes passing at different altitudes.

I see a substantial increase in the use of public commuter airlines rather than owner-user air commuting. . . .

Arthur E. Raymond [engineering chief at Douglas] takes a more optimistic view of the average man's chances of flying his own plane in the year 2000, or even considerably before then:

I think the average man will be using air travel much more generously than now because he will have found it the safest, most expeditious, and cheapest form of transportation. Some form of "convertiplane" will probably have been developed, combining an ability to rise and descend vertically with an ability to attain good normal performance.

I've been thinking that while traffic problems in the air might be great, they might be greater on the ground. The only other thing you could do is burrow into the ground. . . .

None of the experts feel that atomic energy would be useful in private planes by the year 2000.

Shielding passengers from the dangerous gamma rays which are generated would involve heavy walls of lead or other insulator too cumbersome to handle.

Mr. Schmued is alarmed by the possibility of the use of atom power in light planes, in case some lighter insulator could be contrived.

"Everyone is mechanically inclined in the United States," he says. "They'd start tinkering with it and have plenty of trouble." . . .

All of the authorities mention the possibilities that our cities may be dispersed, the population spread out, as an air defense. This dispersal, if it goes into effect, will probably bring into existence a new kind of airline; the short-radius line, the aerial bus, probably some kind of helicopter or convertiplane.

This idealism about the power of aviation is of course counterbalanced by the expected rocky conservatism. Asked what he estimates will be the principal problems of military and civilian aviation fifty years from now, Mr. Raymond replies:

The same as they are now: getting the most in results per dollar of expenditure. I would hope and anticipate that the proportion of effort going into civil aviation would be considerably more than it is now. At least, this is a goal toward which we must all strive.

William Littlewood, American Airlines vice president, engineering, puts it in slightly different language:

The role of aviation during the next fifty years, in a world under capable and successful leadership devoted to the cause of peace, will be to provide more and more transport of men and goods, at substantially increased speeds but at no greater costs; with more dependability, convenience and comport, and with even greater safety.

AND MORE TO COME [7]

The next fifty years of powered flight will make the last seem like slow motion.

Within the next half century, travel time to any place on earth will be negligible.

Even within twenty-five years, all long distance transport will be at supersonic speeds—at speeds greater than seven hundred miles an hour.

And travel to the moon is attainable.

These are the optimistic predictions of a scholarly looking man who wears neat blue suits, shiny black shoes and who occasionally preaches from the pulpit of a downtown Washington church. He is Dr. Hugh L. Dryden, . . . [head of] the National Advisory Committee for Aeronautics (NACA), the top government agency plowing into the heady problems of high-speed, high-altitude flight research.

The NACA does not design or build planes. This is the job of the aircraft industry in trying to meet military or civilian plane requirements. To make tomorrow's planes, aircraft manufacturers use the findings of the NACA as their foundation, and then employ thousands of designers and aerodynamicists on the developmental aspects, as well as engineering specialists in electronics, metallurgy, mechanics and related fields. NACA enters the developmental research field only on request.

Nor does it ordinarily get into applied military plane research, such as armaments, flight instrumentation or aeromedicine. Such matters fall into the bailiwick of the military, unless it asks for a hand.

To keep ahead of the military and the industry's demands for basic information, Dr. Dryden runs a far-flung research empire. Under the close scrutiny of a seventeen-man board of directors, he operates three research centers: the Lewis Propulsion Laboratory at Cleveland and two aerodynamic labs, the Langley Labo-

[7] From "Aviation's Next Fifty Years: As Science Sees Them," article by Alfred Steinberg, magazine writer and political analyst. *Nation's Business.* 41:26-7+. Copyright 1953, reprinted from the December 1953 issue of *Nation's Business.*

ratory in Virginia and the Ames Laboratory in California. The Lewis Lab concentrates on increasing knowledge about engines, especially jets and rockets; while the Langley and Ames Laboratories work on improving the shapes of tomorrow's planes. . . .

All this scientific study is just scratching into the crust of the enormous problems that must be solved before supersonic flying becomes an everyday experience. More and more brain twisters keep cropping up the further scientists get into the field.

One of these, for example, is what can be done to offset surface heating of planes at low-altitude supersonic flying?

In scientific lingo, Mach 1 is the speed of sound, or 760 miles an hour at sea level. At Mach 4, or four times the speed of sound, the heat of the plane's surface will rise to 900 degrees F. At Mach 10 it will rise to 10,000 degrees, which is approximately the heat of the sun.

Today's aluminum alloys lose their strength at about 600 degrees F. But NACA scientists aren't too concerned about this. They will either have to devise an artificial cooling system, use other metals, such as stainless steel or titanium, or make a new type aluminum alloy.

Or take the fuel problem of high-speed, long distance flight.

Petroleum products admittedly occupy too much space and don't release enough energy to meet requirements. Liquid oxygen and hydrogen, atomic energy or fluorine may be the plane fuels of the future. If atomic energy is the answer, scientists will have to find lightweight shields to protect plane occupants from injurious rays.

High-speed flying has further unanswered problems. To reach high Mach numbers, we will need slenderer fuselages and almost paper-thin wings. How can these be made strong enough so that they won't buckle, go into a flutter vibration dance or disintegrate suddenly from fatigue?

New developments in automatic controls are also needed. At high Mach numbers, normal human reaction time makes human direction of the plane impossible or dangerous.

Still another puzzling problem is how to construct a supersonic plane that will fly with equal balance and control in the subsonic and transonic speed ranges. The transonic range lies between 600 and 800 miles per hour.

Supersonic planes have to take off and land at subsonic speeds and have to clear the transonic range both going and coming. At subsonic speeds, the air knows you are coming and deviates from your path. At supersonic speeds, your plane slashes its way through the air. At transonic speeds, a mixture of the two occurs in proportions not as yet determinable. At the exact speed of sound, enormous shock waves, called chokings, occur.

Some designers think that the answer to this problem may come in varying the shape of the sweptback or triangular or delta supersonic wings during the plane's flight. This might be done by altering the sweep angle of the wing at different speeds. Some think it can be done by using flaps, either in the wings or elsewhere.

On the Langley NACA staff, his pockets stuffed with slide rules, is a relaxed, handsome Irishman from Lowell, Massachusetts, named John Stack, who . . . has a good idea of our air potential in the next decade. . . . Mr. Stack goes so far as to say:

1. All combat military planes will be supersonic by 1963. They will travel capably at twice the speed of sound, or faster than the speed with which the earth rotates.

2. On the transport side, supersonic flying will be available, but because of high operating costs, passenger flights across the Atlantic or from coast to coast will probably be made by jet liners in the 550-600-mile-per-hour range. Whether you go to London in two and a half hours by supersonic plane or in five hours in a jet liner will be determined by how much more you will be willing to pay for the extra speed.

In ten years, supersonic planes probably still will be immense eaters of fuel. As a result, they will carry mostly fuel and will not be able to accommodate many passengers.

3. We will be able to go anywhere on the globe nonstop.

4. The supersonic plane of 1963 will be unlike anything we have seen so far. It will probably be made of stainless steel or titanium and will weigh about 200,000 pounds. Its thin narrow wings will be set toward the rear of the long, sleek fuselage. With pressurized cabins, its interior will be fully as comfortable as commercial planes of today.

5. Supersonic seaplanes will be in abundance. Since they take off and land on water, snow and wet sod, the military will be able to scatter its planes and yet have them rendezvous easily.

Supersonic seaplanes are already here, thanks to NACA's development of retractable hydro-skis in cooperation with the Navy and Consolidated-Vultee.

6. We will probably have "vertical risers" by 1963.

The vertical riser combines the vertical ability of the helicopter with the horizontal abilities of the airplane. It will take off and land vertically and fly horizontally at a speed of at least 400 miles per hour. It means we will be able to get in and out of insignificant places, yet fly swiftly. . . .

7. If we improve our guidance, we might be able to shoot mail from New York to Boston by short distance rockets in ten years. . . .

There will probably never be a time when the flight industry will sit back on the proverbial laurels and become static. The performance features that set it off from all other industries are speed and distance. And it has an insatiable appetite to advance both.

We may as well grow accustomed to winging our way with it, no matter what strange planet it leads us to. For as Wilbur Wright put it a long, long time ago:

"We see enough already to be certain that it will be magnificent."

BIBLIOGRAPHY

An asterisk (*) preceding a reference indicates that the article or a part of it has been reprinted in this book.

BOOKS AND PAMPHLETS

Ahnstrom, D. N. Complete book of helicopters. 160p. World Publishing Co. Cleveland, Ohio. '54.

Air France. World's largest airline. 48p. The Company. 683 Fifth Ave. New York 22. '57.

Air Line Pilots Association International. ALPA story. 44p. The Association. 55th St. and Cicero Ave. Chicago 38. '57.

Air Transport Association of America. Air transport facts and figures. 18th ed. 26p. The Association. 1000 Connecticut Ave. Washington 6, D.C. '57.

Air Transport Association of America. Airports manual. 27p. The Association. 1000 Connecticut Ave. Washington 6, D.C. '54.

Air Transport Association of America. American airpower and world aviation; address by Stuart G. Tipton, president of the Association, to the Aero Club of Washington, June 26, 1956. 5p. The Association. 1000 Connecticut Ave. Washington 6, D.C. '56.

*Air Transport Association of America. Career opportunities with the airlines. 75p. The Association. 1000 Connecticut Ave. Washington 6, D.C. '57.

Air Transport Association of America. Elusive airline dollar; address by T. Carl Wedel at Aviation Writers Association Convention, St. Louis, Missouri, May 30, 1957. The Association. 1000 Connecticut Ave. Washington 6, D.C. '57.

Air Transport Association of America. Magic web—the story of your Federal airways. 9p. The Association. 1000 Connecticut Ave. Washington 6, D.C. '57.

Aircraft Industries Association of America. Aviation facts and figures, 1958. 135p. The Association. 1001 Vermont Ave. Washington 5, D.C. '58.

Alexander, H. M. Tomorrow's air age. 248p. Rinehart & Co. New York. '53.

American Airlines. Welcome aboard. 64p. The Company. 100 Park Ave. New York 17. '57.

Armstrong, H. G. Principles and practice of aviation medicine. 496p. Williams & Wilkins. Baltimore. '52.

Balchen, Bernt. Next fifty years of flight. 214p. Harper and Bros. New York. '54.

Baughman's Aviation Dictionary and Reference Guide. 653p. Aero Publishers. Los Angeles. '51.

Benford, R. J. Doctors in the sky. 326p. Charles C. Thomas. Springfield, Ill. '55.

Floherty, J. J. Aviation from shop to sky. 215p. J. B. Lippincott Co. Philadelphia. '41.

Gibbs-Smith, C. H. History of flying. 304p. Frederic A. Praeger. New York. '54.

Gill, F. W. and Bates, G. L. Airline competition. 704p. Harvard University. Graduate School of Business Administration. Division of Research. Boston. '49.

Glidden, H. K. and others. Airports: design, construction, and management. 583p. McGraw-Hill Book Co. New York. '46.

Hardy, A. C. Sky-ships; the story of sky ways and sky trade, past, present, and future. 160p. Nicholson & Watson. London. '43.

Holland, Maurice. Architects of aviation. 213p. Little, Brown & Co. Boston. '51.

Hunsaker, J. C. Aeronautics at the mid-century. 116p. Yale University Press. New Haven, Conn. '52.

International Air Transport Association. Facts about IATA. 12p. The Association. Montreal 3, Quebec. '55.

International Air Transport Association. World air transport statistics, 1957 issue. 40p. The Association. Montreal 3, Quebec. '57.

Jane's All the World's Aircraft, 1957-58. 488p. McGraw-Hill Book Co. New York. '58.

Knight, Clayton and Knight, K. S. Plane crash; the mysteries of major air disasters and how they were solved. 213p. Greenberg, Publisher. New York. '58.

Kysor, H. D. Aircraft in distress: manual of air survival. 428p. Chilton Co. Philadelphia. '55.

Langewiesche, Wolfgang. Flier's world. 278p. McGraw-Hill Book Co. New York. '51.

Leavitt, William and others. Space frontier. 18p. National Aviation Education Council. 1025 Connecticut Ave. Washington 6, D.C. '58.

Lewellen, John. Jet transports. 151p. Thomas Y. Crowell Co. New York. '55.

Leyson, B. W. Wings around the world. 192p. E. P. Dutton & Co. New York. '48.

Mansfield, Harold. Vision. 389p. Duell, Sloan, and Pearce. New York. '56.

Morris, L. R., and Smith, Kendall. Ceiling unlimited: the story of American aviation from Kitty Hawk to supersonics. 417p. Macmillan Co. New York. '53.

National Aviation Education Council. Aircraft number 116, the story of the aircraft plant. 32p. The Council. 1025 Connecticut Ave. Washington 6, D.C. '54.

National Aviation Education Council. Flying cargo. 32p. The Council. 1025 Connecticut Ave. Washington 6, D.C. '56.

National Aviation Education Council. Helicopters. 32p. The Council. 1025 Connecticut Ave. Washington 6, D.C. '54.

National Aviation Education Council. U.S. aviation today, 1958. 123p. The Council. 1025 Connecticut Ave. Washington 6, D.C. '58.

Ogburn, W. F. and others. Social effects of aviation. 755p. Houghton Mifflin Co. Boston. '46.

Ray, Jim. Story of air transport. 104p. John C. Winston Co. Philadelphia. '47.

Ross, Frank, Jr. Flying windmills, the story of the helicopter. 192p. Lothrop, Lee and Shepard. New York. '53.

Shrader, W. A. Fifty years of flight. 178p. Institute of the Aeronautical Sciences. 2 E. 64th St. New York 21. '53.

Smith, H. L. Airways abroad. 355p. University of Wisconsin Press. Madison. '50.

Speas, R. D. Airline operation. 363p. American Aviation Publications. Washington, D.C. '48.

Stillson, Blanche. Wings: insects, birds, men. 299p. Bobbs-Merrill Co. Indianapolis. '54.

Stuart, John. Air travel comes of age. (Public Affairs Pamphlet no 114A). 28p. Public Affairs Committee. 22 E. 38th St. New York 16. '56.

Taylor, J. W. R. Passengers, parcels, and panthers; the story of our working aircraft. Roy Publishers. New York. '56.

United States. Department of Commerce. Air Coordinating Committee. Annual report to the President, 1957. 47p. Supt. of Docs. Washington 25, D.C. '58.

United States. Department of Commerce. Air Coordinating Committee. Convertiplane. 58p. Supt. of Docs. Washington 25, D.C. '54.

*United States. Department of Commerce. Civil Aeronautics Administration. CAA story. 17p. The Department. Washington 25, D.C.

United States. Department of Commerce. Civil Aeronautics Administration. Federal airway plan. Fiscal years 1959-1963. 67p. Supt. of Docs. Washington 25, D.C. '58.

United States. Department of Commerce. Civil Aeronautics Administration. Some ABC's of ATC (Air Traffic Control). 10p. The Department. Washington 25, D.C. '58.

United States. Department of Commerce. Civil Aeronautics Administration. Program Planning Office. 1960-1965-1970 Civil aviation and Federal airways forecasts. 70p. The Department. Washington 25, D.C. '56.

United States. Department of the Air Force. Historical data; a chronology of American aviation events. 114p. The Department. Washington 25, D.C. '55.

United States. President's Air Policy Commission. Survival in the air age; a report. 166p. Supt. of Docs. Washington 25, D.C. '48.

Varney, Alex. Psychology of flight. 269p. D. Van Nostrand Co. New York. '50.

Wilson, G. L. and Bryan, Leslie. Air transportation. 655p. Prentice-Hall. New York. '50.

Wolfe, Thomas. Air transportation; traffic and management. 725p. McGraw-Hill Book Co. New York. '50.

Wood, J. W. Airports and air traffic; the airport needs of your community. 159p. Coward-McCann. New York. '49.

Wright, Orville. How we invented the airplane. 78p. David McKay Co. New York. '53.

PERIODICALS

AMA Archives of Industrial Health. 17:64-6. Ja. '58. Role of the flight surgeon in aviation safety. C. E. Wilbur.

AMA Archives of Industrial Health. 17:111-17. F. '58. Prevention of death and injury in aircraft accidents. H. C. Moseley and others.

AMA Archives of Industrial Health. 17:170-3. F. '58. Health preventive aspects of aviation medicine in a commercial airline operation. O. B. Schreuder.

Aero Digest. 61:33-47+. Ag. '50. Quarter century of distinguished achievement. I. F. Angstadt and others.

*Air Force. 39:117-21. Je. '56. Aerial lifeline in reserve. M. W. Arnold.

Air Line Pilot. 25:9-11+. Ja. '56. 25 years of working conditions. A. P. Holman.

American Aviation. 20:93-4. F. 11, '57. Political pressure makes life difficult for CAB. M. V. Henzey.

American Aviation. 20:76-7. F. 25, '57. Twin headaches: no-shows and oversale. Eric Bramley.

American Aviation. 20:74. My. 6, '57. High court ruling spells finis for Trans American.

American Aviation. 21:59-60. Jl. 1, 1957. Russian TU-104: impressive but no money maker. Anthony Vandyk.

American Aviation. 21:85-6. Jl. 17, '57. Should U.S. guarantee loans to small airlines?

American Aviation. 21:43. Ap. 7, '58. Jet age problems worry unions.

American Aviation. 21:35-7. Ap. 21, '58. CAA's 20th anniversary: celebration or wake?

American Aviation. 21:42-4. Ap. 21, '58. Ground support: carriers' cost headache. George Hart.

*American Aviation. 21:39-40. My. 5, '58. MATS: Pentagon's air transport monster. Robert Burkhardt.

American Aviation. 21:25-6. My. 19, '58. Look ahead at FAA's potential. Robert Burkhardt.

American Aviation. 22:41-3. Je. 16, '58. Inside story of the aviation act. Robert Burkhardt.

American City. 67:92-3. Ja. '52. Municipal planning for helicopters. C. M. Belinn.

American City. 72:159+. Ag. '57. Downtown heliports.

American Economic Review. 42:103-25. Mr. '52. Domestic airline self-sufficiency: a problem of route structure. H. D. Koontz.

American Mercury. 77:38-40. S. '53. Queer cargoes by air. Trevor Holloway.

American Mercury. 81:109-13. D. '55. Fight for air routes. George Carroll.

American Mercury. 84:57-62. Ja. '57. Cargo in the clouds. J. H. Winchester.

American Mercury. 87:17-21. Jl. '58. Red stars in our skies; reciprocal air service between the U.S. and Russia? George Carroll.

American Mercury. 87:65-8. Jl. '58. Ohio's backyard air line. Noel Wical.

Architectural Forum. 108:122-9. D. '57. Airports for tomorrow.

Architectural Forum. 108:79-87. F. '58. New aerial gateway to America; report on Idlewild.

*Atlantic Monthly. 192:37-41. Ag. '53. Freighters of the future. Robert Gross and W. W. Haines.

Atlantic Monthly. 200:89-94. O. '57. Future of flight. L. N. Ridenour.

*Atlantic Monthly. 200:118-19. O. '57. Traffic control in crowded skies. E. P. Curtis.

Aviation Week. 66:59-73. F. 11, '57. Russians criticize Stalinist air history.
    Translation from *Voprosy Istorii,* official Russian historical journal.

Aviation Week. 66:1-322. F. 25, '57. Twenty-fourth annual inventory of airpower.
    Entire issue.

Aviation Week. 68:48-67. Ja. 20, '58. Boeing seeks to lead jet age market with 707s. Richard Sweeney.

Aviation Week. 68:38-9. Ja. 27, '58. Airlines prod board for higher fares. L. L. Doty.

Aviation Week. 68:38-40. F. 17, '58. Soviets may offer TU-114 to world market.

Aviation Week. 68:36-7. F. 24, '58. CAA wins battle for airspace control. L. L. Doty.

Aviation Week. 68:1-344. Mr. 3, '58. Twenty-fifth annual inventory of airpower.
    Entire issue.

Aviation Week. 68:38-9. Ap. 7, '58. Financial crisis hits all-cargo airlines. Glenn Garrison.

Aviation Week. 68:77+. Ap. 14, '58. CAB accident investigation report: pilot blamed in Rikers Island crash; ALPA protests board's findings.

Aviation Week. 69:28-9. Ag. 11, '58. President receives airline aid proposal (Quesada report).

*Barron's. 35:13-14. S. 12, '55. Flying taxis. Norris Willatt.

*Bee-Hive [United Aircraft Corporation]. 32:2-15. Fall '57. Quick and nimble carriers.

Business Week. p 143-54. Ja. 31, '53. Taxi plane: missing link in air travel.

Business Week. p92-4+. My. 1, '54. Airports turn to the engineers.

Business Week. p50-2. Ag. 13, '55. Flying green goods to market.

*Business Week. p 156-70. Jl. 21, '56. With the whoosh of the jets the airlines grow up.

*Business Week. p32-6. D. 29, '56. For feeder airlines it's a lot of work for low pay.

Business Week. p41-3. Je. 15, '57. Industry braces for the big change.

Business Week. p 177+. S. 14, '57. Too big for its own good.

Business Week. p 112-14+. N. 9, '57. Whirly-birds go for do-it-yourself market.

*Business Week. p90-2+. N. 30, '57. Dream of jet age airports still far from reality.

Business Week. p23-4. Je. 7, '58. Averting collisions in the air.

*Collier's. 130:15-18. Ag. 2, '52. Air-crash detective at work. Richard Witkin.

*Collier's. 138:26-36. Ag. 31, '56. Our crowded sky. T. H. White.

Collier's. 138:39-45. Ag. 31, '56. Russia's edge in jetliners. J. I. Haggerty, Jr.

Coronet. 38:72-6. Je. '55. First plane across the U.S.A. Tom Mahoney.

Flying. 57:34-5+. O. '55. Passengers pioneered, too. H. J. Hayes.

Flying. 59:36-7+. D. '56. Thirteen feeders. J. H. Winchester.

Fortune. 44:87-92+. D. '51. Big money airline.

Fortune. 53:118-20+. Ja. '56. Twelve thousand company planes. Spencer Klaw.

Fortune. 53:91-5+. F. '56. Airlines' flight from reality. D. A. Saunders.

Fortune. 54:112-13+. Jl. '56. What the airlines expect from the 1961 jet fleet. C. R. Smith.

*Fortune. 54:144-8+. S. '56. Price of air safety. E. L. Van Deusen.

Fortune. 56:129-33+. O. '57. Selling of the 707.

Fortune. 56:165-78. D. '57. Search for the ultimate fuel. G. A. W. Boehm.

*Fortune. 57:136-7+. Mr. '58. VTOL: the next way to fly. Francis Bello.

*Fortune. 67:120-4+. Je. '58. International airlines: the great jet gamble.

Harper's Magazine. 206:25-33. Je. '53. How we invented the airplane. Orville Wright.

Harper's Magazine. 213:40-5. S. '56. Russian roulette on our airways? Ernest Conine.

Harper's Magazine. 215:74-6. S. '57. Jet that crashed before take-off.
Beirne Lay, Jr.
  Same condensed. Reader's Digest. 71:65-8. N. '57.
Harper's Magazine. 217:72-4. Ag. '58. Gadget to cut down on mid-air
collisions. A. M. Watkins.
Holiday. 23:66-7+. Je. '58. Hostess on flight 408. P. E. Deutschman.
Life. 44:28-30. Je. 2, '58. Crisis in the sky; congested air and collision.
Life. 45:68-77. Ag. 25, '58. Glamor girls of the air.
Mechanical Engineering. 28:28-9+. Mr. '58. Aviation's golden age;
evaluation of the fabulous period from 1940 to 1960. J. E. Forry.
Nation. 185:401-5, 428-31. N. 30-D. 7, '57. Airpower lobby. Al
Toffler.
National Council Outlook. 6:6-7+. O. '56. Flying parsons. Geraldine
Sartain.
National Geographic Magazine. 104:721-56. D. '53. Aviation looks
ahead on its 50th birthday. E. S. Land.
National Geographic Magazine. 104:757-80. D. '53. Fact finding for
tomorrow's planes. H. L. Dryden.
National Geographic Magazine. 111:283-317. Mr. '57. MATS: Amer-
ica's long arm of the air. B. M. Bowie.
*Nation's Business. 41:25-9+. D. '53. Aviation's next 50 years: as
science sees them. Alfred Steinberg; As industry sees them. Richard
Tregaskis.
*Nation's Business. 44:29-31+. Je. '56. Military airline outgrows them
all.
New York Herald Tribune. sec 2, p 1. Jl. 21, '57. Acute U.S. air traffic
problem: a report. Don Irwin and others.
*New York Times. p X21. N. 17, '57. Air fare hearing to open.
P. J. C. Friedlander.
New York Times. p85. Je. 1, '58. New helicopters likened to DC-3's.
Richard Witkin.
New York Times Magazine. p 11+. Jl. 15, '56. To promote safety in
the air. W. B. Harding.
New York Times Magazine. p24. F. 17, '57. Detective story: why did
the plane crash? C. B. Palmer.
Newsweek. 41:84-5. Ja. 19, '53. Anything to the ends of the earth by
air freight.
Newsweek. 50:76+. Jl. 15, '57. Who flies where?
Newsweek. 50:58-60. Ag. 5, '57. Conquest of the air.
*Newsweek. 50:86-7. O. 21, '57. Nobody wants to wait. J. A. Con-
way.
Public Utilities Fortnightly. 58:899-906. D. 6, '56. Developments in
irregular air-carrier operations. L. L. Stentzel.
Reader's Digest. 68:109-12. Mr. '56. Flying Fish, ace airline detec-
tive. Lawrence Lader.

*Reader's Digest. 69:49-53. Jl. '56. Big traffic jam in the sky. Wolf-
gang Langewiesche.
    Condensed from Air Facts. Je. '56.
Reader's Digest. 69:27-30. N. '56. Here come the commercial jets with
a whoosh!
Reader's Digest. 69:188-9+. N. '56. I knew the Wright brothers were
crazy. A. W. Drinkwater.
*Reader's Digest. 72:134-5+. Mr. '58. Man who wrote DC in the sky.
Francis and Katharine Drake.
*Reader's Digest. 73:58-62. Jl. '58. Let's ride the new jet liner.
Wolfgang Langewiesche.
    Condensed from Harper's Magazine. 216:50-6. Je. '58. New jet air
liners.
Reporter. 15:30-3. Ag. 9, '56. Of space and time, and death in the air.
L. H. Berlin.
*Reporter. 16:29-34. My. 30, '57. Rise and fall of the nonskeds.
Robert Bendiner.
SAE [Society of Automotive Engineers] Journal. 66:70-1. N. '57. Re-
quirements for airports of the future. M. A. Warskow.
Saturday Evening Post. 226:25+. D. 26, '53. Those lost-luggage
mysteries. Henry LaCossitt.
*Saturday Evening Post. 226:24-5+. Je. 26, '54. Adventures of the
air-line stewardesses. Henry LaCossitt.
Saturday Evening Post. 229:46-7+. S. 29, '56. Los Angeles to New
York in four hours. P. H. Gustafson.
Saturday Evening Post. 229:23+. N. 10, '56. Flying can be safer.
H. H. Martin.
Saturday Review. 40:19-20+. Ja. 12, '57. Travelers raise the storm
signal. Horace Sutton.
Science Digest. 38:37-41. D. '55. What it takes to be an airline pilot.
    Excerpt from First five million miles. 276p. Harper and Bros. New
York. '55.
Science Digest. 43:77-82. My. '58. Search for the perfect aircraft.
J. L. B. Blizard.
Senior Scholastic. 72:16-18. My. 9, '58. Our "Model-T" airways.
*Time. 47:77-86. Ja. 14, '46. Salesman at work.
Time. 71:90. My. 19, '58. International airlines: many should stay
home.
U.S. News & World Report. 40:48-51. Ja. 20, '56. Jet age ahead—
airports lag.
U.S. News & World Report. 41:34-5. Jl. 13, '56. U.S. skies getting
overcrowded.
U.S. News & World Report. 42:77-8+. My. 3, '57. Is air travel
moving into first place?
U.S. News & World Report. 43:105-8. N. 22, '57. Now it's the airlines
in trouble.

U.S. News & World Report. 44:89-92. Ap. 11, '58. Jetliners around the corner but no place to land.

Westinghouse Engineer. 17:178-80. N. '57. Aviation communications and navigation; today and tomorrow. F. B. Gunter and N. B. Tharp.

World Air Transport Background [International Air Transport Association]. 1956, no.2. How international airline fares and rates are made.

Tyler, Poyntz, *ed.*
　　Airways of America.　New York, H. W. Wilson Co., 1958.

　　189 p.　21 cm.　(The　Reference shelf, v. 30, no. 6)

　　　1. Aeronautics, Commercial—U. S.　2. Air traffic control—U. S.
I. Title.

TL521.T9　　　　　　　　　387.7082　　　　　　　58–12647 ‡

Library of Congress

──────────

387.7　Tyler, Poyntz,　　　　　　　ed.
　　　Airways of America.　Wilson, H.W. 1958
　　　189p (Reference shelf v30, no.6)

　　　This book "is concerned solely with the airplane as an instrument of
trade and commerce and with the men and women who have made it—in
little more than half a century—the predominant means of public transportation in the United States."　Preface
　　　Bibliography: p181-89

　　1　Aeronautics, Commercial　I Title　II Series　　　　　　387.7

58W3639　　　　　　　　　　　(W)　The H. W. Wilson Company